Oleg Gokov

Imperial Russia and the Shah's Iran: common problems of history

Oleg Gokov

Imperial Russia and the Shah's Iran: common problems of history

Late 18th - 20th centuries

ScienciaScripts

Cover image: www.ingimage.com

This book is a translation from the original published under ISBN 978-613-9-84045-8.

Publisher:
Sciencia Scripts
is a trademark of
Dodo Books Indian Ocean Ltd. and OmniScriptum S.R.L publishing group

120 High Road, East Finchley, London, N2 9ED, United Kingdom
Str. Armeneasca 28/1, office 1, Chisinau MD-2012, Republic of Moldova, Europe
Printed at: see last page
ISBN: 978-620-6-30045-8

Table of Contents

Introduction

The late 18th and early 20th centuries were a turning point in the fate of Eurasia. This is the time when the Industrial Revolution and the Western model of society spread around the world, incorporating peoples, societies and states into the orbit of the Eurocentric world. The included reacted to these changes in different ways. But what they generally had in common was that those that were able to adapt and transform survived and developed, while those that took the transformation hard became dependent on the stronger and more successful.

In this context, the example of two neighbors - Russia and Iran - is interesting. Their response to Western expansion was different. The results were also different. By the outbreak of the First World War in 1914-1918, Russia was in a financially dependent position, but in the ranks of the West. Russia was financially dependent but among the advanced powers. Iran, on the other hand, was almost completely dependent on Russia and Great Britain.

In the three articles of this collection we examine some issues of comparative development and interaction between the Russian Empire and Iran during the late 18th and early 20th centuries. Particular attention is paid to military issues, since both in Iran and Russia the armed forces were at the cutting edge of modernization. Russia actively participated in the Europeanization of the Iranian army since the last third of the 19th century.

1. The Russian Empire and Qajar Iran: the common and the special

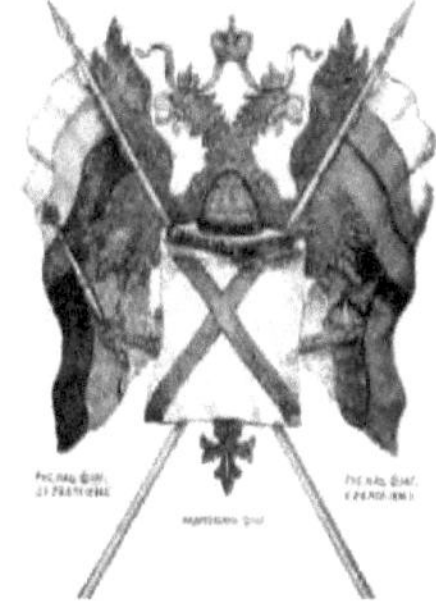

Russian flags before and after April 29, 1896.[1]

Iranian flag from the reign of Nasreddin Shah (1848-1896)

Russia and Iran have long-standing interstate relations. Before the First World War of 1914-1918, they developed most intensively from the late 18th to the first quarter of the 20th centuries. In recent decades, the topic of studying and comparing empires has become very popular. However, as a rule, Russia is compared with European powers and the Ottoman Empire, and not always correctly[2] . At the same time, the Iranian problematic has always been and still is on the second or even third plan of researchers. But Russia and Persia (so in XIX - first third of XX centuries in Europe called Iran[3]) were neighbors for a long time, both were empires by their structure[4] . It is all the more interesting to see what these states had in common and what was special.

State emblems of Persia under the Qajars

The Great State Emblem of the Russian Empire

Many things united the empires. Both of them had long been known to Europe under exonyms that had never been used within these powers - Persia and Muscovy. But if the first name was the result of the ancient tradition, on which the Western European culture was based since the Renaissance, the second was the result of a propaganda campaign on the part of the Polish-Lithuanian Commonwealth, whose representatives deliberately called Muscovite Russia and then the Russian state Moscovia, thus denying the legitimacy of the struggle of Ivan III[5] and his successors for the reunification of the lands of Kievan Rus[6] .

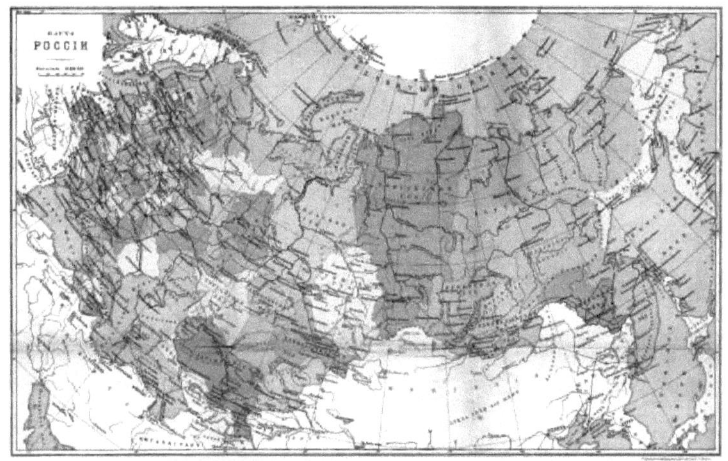

Map of the Russian Empire at the end of the 19th century.

Early 20th century map of Persia.

Another factor uniting the two monarchies is the principle of empire handed down over the centuries. In Iran it had older roots - from the Achaemenid power (VI-IV centuries BC) and was embodied in the title "Shahanshah" ("King of Kings") and the concept of "Iran" as something supra-ethnic and supra-religious, symbolizing the supreme power, empire[7] . In Russia, imperial motifs appeared around the 15th century[8] . The symbolism of the royal power of Russian sovereigns combined Byzantine,

Golden Horde (or nomadic), Roman and Old Russian imperial motifs[9] . Here the emphasis was on religious and power continuity, first from ancient Rome, then from Byzantium, with an emphasis on the tsar as the center of the imperial system[10] . Both Russia and Iran were ruled by non-ethnic dynasties[11] . True, in Russia the dynasty was Germanized by blood, but in spirit it remained Russian. Besides, it was legitimate in the eyes of the ordinary population and sanctified by the religious doctrine of Orthodoxy. In Iran, though the Qajar Turks adopted the Persian culture (including the state administration), they remained a foreign element. It was connected with the peculiarities of the Shiite doctrine of the state, where the role of the monarch was only temporary, and with the fact that among the nomadic tribes there were long-lasting claims to the central power, which was still relatively recently (in the 18th century) held in their hands by Afshars, Zendas and others. Besides, as the Armenian philologist Garnik Serobovich Asatryan noted, "for Iranian politicians - regardless of their origin .... the priorities of the Iranian state have never been overshadowed by any parochial interests"[12] .

M.A. Zini. Alexander II and Shah Nasreddin during a parade on Tsaritsyny Meadow in 1873 (both Russian flags and one of the flags of Iran under Nasreddin Shah are shown here).

The religious outlook of a significant part of the population and the ideology of both states was characterized by messianism. In Russia it was the aspiration to unite under the rule of the Orthodox monarch and the Orthodox Church all Orthodox Christians (later - and the Slavs), to return Constantinople and make the Russian state really the "Third Rome" - the spiritual and religious center of true believers. Iran, on the other hand, since Safavid times[13] was the only country in the Islamic world where Shiism held dominant positions. This position as the center of Shiism also conditioned foreign policy claims of Iranian rulers, in particular, the struggle for Turkish Iraq with its Shiite shrines. At the same time, the dream of the Qajar monarchs, up to and including Nasreddin Shah, was to recreate the state of Nadir Shah Afshar and the succession of the former dynasties that ruled in Iran[14] .

Symbols of the Russian monarchy: two coronation hats - "Cap of Monomakh" and "Cap of Kazan"; crowns of the Emperor and Empress, orb, scepter and chain

What Russia and Iran had in common was a multi-structured economy. It is true that the Romanov Empire was far ahead of its rival in the transition to capitalism.

Persian monarchs Agha Mohammad Shah, Fathali Shah and Mohammadali Shah with Shah regalia: wearing different crowns and with a sword consecrated on the tomb of Sheikh Sefiaddin in the

Ardebile. Fathali Shah is wearing the symbolic crown of Nadir Shah

Both empires were characterized by multi-ethnic and multi-confessional (multi-religious) composition of the population with the presence of a predominant confession: Orthodoxy in Russia and Shiism in Iran. At the same time, the titular peoples were in approximately the same position: formally - the first, actually - living no better than others. In Persia, however, there was a specificity. In Russia, the Russian people comprising Great Russians, Belorussians and Malorussians constituted the "imperial ethnos"[15] . In Iran, the Iranians proper - the titular ethnos - occupied a secondary position in comparison with the ethnos from which the ruling dynasty originated. Iranians (Persians) constituted a significant part of the urban population, engaged mainly in trade, usury and agriculture. Although a few battalions of regular infantry were formed from them, they were mostly exempted from military service. In fact, the "imperial" people were the Turks of Iranian Azerbaijan and Iraq- Ajemi, who were mainly engaged in agriculture[16] . They formed the backbone of the regular army, which testified not only to their personal qualities as "good military material", but also to the fact that the ruling dynasty preferred to initially rely on their tribesmen[17] . Both in Russia, the Russians and in Iran, the Turks of Azerbaijan and Iraq-Ajami were mostly dependent on their landlords to varying degrees[18] . In both states, they did not exercise the functions of a dominant (dominant) ethnos, as was the case in the Western empires, but were the superior, or titular, ethnos. But by the beginning of the 20th century, nationalism began to play an increasingly important role in both countries. In addition to "small" nationalisms, "imperial" varieties of it grew up here: Russian with the central idea of Orthodoxy and Iranian, with the overriding idea of Shiism[19] . Both of them had an ethno-religious basis. It should be noted that for a long time the terms "Russian" and "Orthodox" (cf.: "Russian faith"), as well as "Iranian" ("Persian") and "Shiite" meant the same thing, respectively. That is, the ethnic component was substituted for the religious component, and the latter played the primary role. But now the ethnic component comes first. At the same time, the supporters of "imperial" nationalisms expressed claims for domination in their own state.

Mikhail Fedorovich Romanov with tsar regalia

Г. Becker. Coronation of Emperor Alexander III and Empress Maria Feodorovna

Nicholas II with regalia of imperial power

Common to both societies was the overriding role of the community in the life of both societies.

However, in Iran communal relations covered both town and village, while in Russia only the village. However, by the end of the 19th century, under the influence of capitalist relations, the community gradually stratified and "eroded".

But there were also significant differences between the states. The main thing that catches the eye is the difference in development. The Russian state, even if we trace its history back to the new Romanov dynasty, had more than 200 years of development and no less than 100 years of modernization experience, it can be safely called "established". Its structures were characterized by "established", relative stability. The Qajar dynasty established itself on the throne after several decades of instability only by the beginning of the XIX century, and the state here was "young", did not have the same durability as in Russia. Despite modernization efforts, Iran lagged far behind the Russian Empire in the sphere of renewal and transfer of its structures to European rails[21] . Thus, if the Russian Empire can be called a traditional bourgeois empire, Persia by the early 20th century remained a classical traditional monarchy with a slight European flavor.

The Bone Throne of Ivan IV and the Throne of Alexander III

Thrones of the Qajar monarchs (the second is the so-called "Peacock Throne")

There were other differences as well. First, in Russia the dynasty was established and legitimate in the eyes of the majority of the population, while in Iran the Qajars' power was largely held on the position of Great Britain and Russia. Secondly, the system of government in Russia was established and dynamic. In Iran, the system existed, but directly depended on the ruler: with the change of the Shah, practically the entire top management apparatus changed. Moreover, the frequent change of managers in Iran was connected with the trade of positions. The shah and lower-ranking managers, seeking material gain, often sold posts to the one who would make a larger contribution to their pockets. Moreover, the terms for which they sold managerial positions were not regulated by any laws or agreements. Therefore, the most permanent ruling elite were the descendants of the Shah's family and the lower ranks of government - khans, ilkhans, etc., heads of tribes, villages, etc., who were the leaders of tribes and villages. In this context, the third difference should also be noted: the unequal value of elites[22] . Two cultures were formed in Russia: elite (i.e., nobility, intellectuals) and popular. They differed significantly from each other. The transition from the bottom to the top was possible, but not too easy. In addition, a stable, though not too numerous bureaucracy was formed here, as well as the all-imperial aristocracy (i.e. the aristocracy and nobility proper), which was rather monolithic. At the same time, there was a lot left over from traditional society in the Russian political elite, which produced a very peculiar fusion. However, it was quite effective. In Iran, on the other hand, components of traditional structures and thinking prevailed. The tribal and regional nobility coexisted with the "administrative" nobility appointed by the Shah and his sons. As a result, there coexisted a hierarchy of office and a hierarchy of personal relations in the form of vassalage. Often both types of nobility overlapped. Common imperial aristocracy was not formed here. The elite consisted of the ruling dynasty, the bureaucracy appointed by the Shah, the communal-clan upper class and the clergy. Constant movements from the bottom to the top and back were quite common. Here nobility did not play such a role as in Russia, because at the will of the Shah (or people close to him) any noble person (heads of tribes, village "landlords", etc.) could be mixed with mud, and an unknown descendant of water carriers could become the head of the Isfahan army or the first minister. This mobility of Persia's political elite largely determined the instability of its development. Besides, in Russia the bourgeoisie was actively forming, whereas in Iran, in the presence of a peculiar organization of power, it was dangerous to be rich[23] . This hindered the formation of a new socio-economic class that played a determining role in European development.

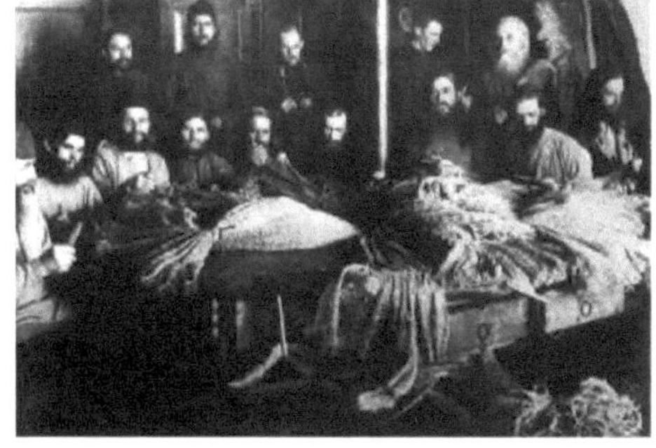

Russian clergy

Iran's Shia clergy

Fourth, the level of loyalty of the ruling elites and various communities (ethnic, tribal, religious, etc.) to the central government in Russia was high, while the Tehran government was disliked even by its most loyal subjects.

Iranian peasants

Russian peasants

The fifth feature of the difference was the formation of the body of the state itself. While Russia's borders were established, as a rule, by representatives of the empire itself, Iran's borders were formalized in the 19th century by external forces. The Tehran government was only forced to sign the relevant documents, recognizing what had been determined without or with its formal participation[24] .

Thus, the Russian Empire and Qajar Iran had many common features. But there were also significant differences, which led to the fact that by the beginning of the 20th century Persia was partially economically and politically dependent on Russia. Persia was partially economically and politically dependent on Russia. These are different socio-economic systems. While Russia was transforming into an industrial-agrarian country during the 19th century, Iran remained an agrarian country dominated by traditional relations. This is the strong role of the clergy in Iran, which hindered economic and social changes in the country. This is also the disinterest in real changes according to the European model of both the ruling elite of Persia and the majority of its population. It is also a longer history of development of the Russian state, which has gone from traditional to industrial-traditional a long way. The Qajar Persia, on the other hand, was a "young" state, which, before it had time to take shape, had already faced the expansion of more economically and politically developed states.

2. General problems of the history of reforming the army of Qajar Iran until the 1870s.

For a long time, the zone of Central and West Asia remained a place of clash of interests and direct contact between three major states - the Ottoman Empire, Russia and Persia[25] . The constant wars between them for supremacy in the region required, among other things, the presence of numerous and capable armies. The factor of military power remained decisive in this confrontation until the 20th century. And while Russia eventually became a powerful state, the influence of the Ottoman Empire and Persia gradually declined, and eventually they became semi-colonies of European countries. This decline was especially pronounced in Persia. Having been one of the great powers of Asia at the dawn of the New Age, it lost its status catastrophically fast by the beginning of the 19th century. Without going deeply into the reasons for this decline, it should be noted that they were rooted in the worldview and socio-economic planes. The situation of the army was a vivid manifestation of the socio-economic and political processes that were taking place in the country, as well as the mentality of its population. Remaining traditional in its essence, i.e. based on tribal and patronage ties, without a clear structure, legislative base, unified armament, etc., it was significantly inferior to the European troops and even the Ottoman army, modernized according to the European model. This was evidenced by the wars of the first half of the 19th century.

The problem of the transfer of military traditions, Europeanization or modernization of the armies of the East has recently often attracted the attention of researchers[26] . There is no doubt that the Eastern rulers, seeing the successes of European armies, or the armies of their neighbors modernized according to the European model, also sought to update their own armed forces, often inviting European military instructors or advisers for this purpose. The creation of regular armed forces[27] , which depended on the central government, occurred in New Age Persia under Abbas 1[28] and Nadir Shah Afshar[29] . However, they were based on the tribal principle of manning and subsequently (as a rule, after the death of the reformer) slowly declined, as the following rulers did not find interest in their qualitative development (improvement of weapons, organization, etc.). At the beginning of the XIX century the Iranian army was mostly irregular, i.e. it had no permanent organization, but was manned by tribal militias when necessary[30] . Therefore, its loyalty to the central government depended on the loyalty of nomadic tribal leaders. The economic-political system caused the fact that already at the beginning of the XIX century Persia was far behind the leading European countries in almost all indicators, including in military affairs. Feudal wars of the 18th century, despotic rule with simultaneous weakness of the central authority in some regions, vertical patron-client ties in society, traditional thinking due to the preserving role of religion - all this did not contribute to development. The changes in military art, which took place in Europe during the XVII-XVIII centuries and were called, in our opinion, "military revolution"[31] , did not affect Iranian lands much by the XIX century. By the beginning of the century innovations penetrated into Iran indirectly through the Ottoman Empire, but they did not stimulate significant development: the Iranian army remained largely at the level of the Safavid army[32] . This applied to the training of soldiers, weapons, and the structure of the armed forces, which were divided into regular and irregular, with the latter making up the majority.

Images of soldiers and officers of the Persian regular army of the early 19th century.

The history of the Iranian army of the New Age was a succession of cycles of transformations, associated primarily with the rise to power of ambitious rulers who aimed at strengthening their own power and extending it over as large a territory as possible. This cycle consisted of the following components: creation (or re-creation) of a regular army (of infantry, cavalry guards-guards and artillery) in opposition to the tribal militias of large feudal lords and rearming it with the most modern weapons at that time - success of the new army in the time of the reformer - decline after his death. Such a cycle can be traced back to the times of Abbas I, Nadir Shah Afshar, and in the 19th century. - under Abbas Mirza[33] and Nasreddin Shah[34] (three times).

Images of soldiers and officers of the Persian regular army of the early 19th century.

In our opinion, the increase in the number of cycles during the reign of the Qajars (4 in one century) is due to the fact that from the beginning of the 19th century Persia began to face European troops on a regular basis and also became actively involved in European politics as a bargaining chip in the struggle between Russia, England and France. The inability to confront the Europeans (primarily the Russians, with whom there were constant wars over Transcaucasia in the first half of the 19th century) on an equal footing and military defeats by them contributed to the emergence of an understanding among some of Persia's dignitaries of the need for fundamental changes. In the 19th century, the cycle of changes in the armed forces of the Qajar state reached a new level. What was new was that European models began to be adopted directly from the original, rather than indirectly through the Ottoman Empire, Russia, or adventurers of European origin (the British under Anthony and Robert Shirley (Shirley) in the time of Abbas I), as had been the case before. The use of European instructors became a regular feature, and changes were made to the principle of building the armed forces (introduction of charters, a clear structure, etc.). In addition, the Europeans themselves, first of all the British and the French, and later the Russians, who replaced the latter in the struggle for influence in Central and West Asia, were to some extent interested in these changes.

پرچمدار درفش دورة عباس میرزا – دوران قاجاریه
Porteur du drapeau d'Abbas Mirza. Epoque Kadjar
Standard-bearer of Abbas Mirza's army, Qajar period

افسر دورة عباس میرزا – دوران قاجاریه
Officier sous les ordres d'Abbas Mirza. Epoque Kadjar
Officer of Abbas Mirza's army, Qajar period

Images of soldiers and officers of the Persian regular army of the early 19th century.

Invitation of European instructors, purchase of weapons in Europe, and attempts to reorganize the armed forces in the European manner were half-successful. The Qajar rulers saw the Europeans (mainly the British and the French) as allies in the struggle against the Russian Empire, and the latter, in turn, saw Iran as an auxiliary country in the struggle among themselves. Under these circumstances, the armed forces of the Qajar monarchy had to divert the enemy's forces, serving the strategic goals of France or Great Britain, which, of course, did not provide for the creation of a really combat-ready Persian army (especially since it could later become a hindrance to the invasive plans of European powers in the Near and Middle East). In addition, it was possible to sell obsolete and dilapidated weapons at inflated prices, which the Europeans did quite successfully during the 19th century.

Zamburek and Zamburekchi (early 19th c.)

Domestic conditions, both economic-political and mental, were not conducive to the development of military affairs. The absence of strong social structures that would be interested in radical changes (like the European bourgeoisie), the attitude of officials to power as a means of enrichment, the lack of a sense of state interest in most of them and in the population in general, and the preserving influence of religion - these factors significantly hindered all attempts to carry out reforms that had been initiated by Abbas-Mirza.

Traditional feudal structures in the form of local nobility, privileged strata (kajars, muhajirs), and clergy, fearing for the stability of their position, resisted any changes. Even the strong Shah's power could not do anything, as its strength largely depended on their position. The fact is that Iran was a country where the majority of the population practiced Shi'ism. The Soviet historian M.A. Igamberdiyev noted that "in Iran representatives of this kind (Qajars - O.G.) were despised by the people as enemies by faith"[35] . As the reasons for this he considered that the representatives of the ruling Qajar dynasty were Sunnis, and even led their lineage from the murderers of Husayn - the son of the fourth "righteous caliph" Ali and the daughter of the Prophet Muhammad Fatima, who was honored by Shiites as a holy martyr[36] . Some of the Qajar tribesmen indeed practiced Sunni Islam, but the bulk were Shiites. Rather, the reasons for the attitude of the population to the Shahs of the Qajar dynasty should be sought in another plane - in the peculiarities of the religious and political doctrine of Shiism. According to this doctrine, only the descendants of the Prophet Muhammad's son-in-law Ali (Alida) have the legitimate right to rule over the faithful (imamate). Since the 12th Imam, according to tradition, disappeared in the IX century to appear later in the form of a messiah, his functions are temporarily performed by ulema and mujtehids - religious scholars, theologians[37] . If the Safavids were descended from the 7th Imam, the dynasties that succeeded them did not have such a "privilege" and were regarded as usurpers[38] . In fact, the Qajar dynasty was also considered as such. Therefore, the authority of it and its rulers in the eyes of the Shi'ite population and clergy largely depended on how zealously they upheld Shi'ite tenets. Hence the Shiite clergy's great power over the believers and the lack of a firm foothold for the Shah's regime in the country. The unpopularity of the ruling dynasty in Persia conditioned the fact that its rulers, in order to strengthen their own power, constantly sought help from Europeans, making significant concessions to them, and were suspicious of intelligent and too energetic people around them. All this made it impossible to build and implement long-term reform projects.

Images of soldiers of the Persian regular army of the early 19th century.

The most vividly stated theses are confirmed by the example of transformations in military affairs, which were attempted in Iran in the mid-19th century. The military reform of Mirza Taghi-khan[39] laid the foundation for the organization of regular armed forces of the Persian state of the considered time, but it was not brought to its logical conclusion. In 1851, on his initiative, the first Persian military statute was adopted and put into effect, which was modeled on the statutes of the English and French armies. It provided for the introduction of a clear organizational structure, defined the procedure for appointment and dismissal of commanders, and envisaged compulsory military exercises and the creation of a trained reserve. To replenish the army with personnel, a system of recruitment was introduced - "boniche" (from the Persian "boneh" ("household", "yard", "family"); this was the name given in then Persia to economic associations of peasant families, which were units of taxation[40]). According to the statute, the Shah was the commander-in-chief of the army as a whole, and the highest command staff was appointed by him and the next most important person after him, the emir-nizam. The armed forces of the empire were to number 50 infantry regiments[41] , 12 cavalry battalions, and 27,000 artillerymen. Regular units were divided into two armies: Iranian and Azerbaijani[42] . Each was headed by separate commanders-in-chief. The military structure was based on the fouj, a regiment[43] , which was headed by a sarkhang. The fouj, in turn, was subdivided into 10 deste (companies) headed by sultans (captains), and its strength was set at 1,000 men. 2 foujes constituted a brigade - type. The brigades were combined into tumani (divisions, or corps): 5 brigades were headed by an emir-penj, and 6-10 by an emir-tumani. The regular cavalry was to consist of the personal guard of the Shah and the heir to the throne - the Ghulams (400 men). The militia, or irregular army, was supposed to consist of infantry and cavalry. Unlike the regular forces, the infantry played a minor role in it. It consisted of detachments of 50-100 men, which were to serve within their area. Cavalry, as before the reform, was to be formed from nomadic tribes. The chiefs of tribes were obliged to show up for public service with a fully equipped detachment at the request of the government. 50-100 cavalrymen constituted a detachment-deste, and 1,000 a fouj. All expenses of the militia were borne by the tribes, for which they, in turn, were exempted from paying maliat (taxes)[44] .

Persian sarbazi in the mid-19th century (1850s, Italian photographer Luigi Pesce)

As we can see, the ideas laid down in the reform of the military system by Mirza Tati-khan were quite productive. However, after his removal from power in 1851 due to the Shah's concern about the growing popularity of his first minister and resistance to reforms among the local nobility, they were never fully implemented[45] , although the structure of the armed forces proposed by him was retained.

Types of Iranian officers in the mid-nineteenth century.

In the course of the global struggle for spheres of influence and colonies between European states and due to internal problems, Persia in the 19th century became an arena of struggle between Russia and Great Britain. It was in the last third of the 19th century that the country finally turned into a semi-independent state. Apart from economic and political factors, the situation in the army, which had already ceased to exist as a combat-ready force in the second half of the century, contributed to this. In the last third of the 19th century, regular military forces in Persia had only a formal character because of the complex system of feudal relations, weak central authority and total corruption, which permeated all pores of the country's social and political life. Nevertheless, they became an object of struggle between representatives of the great European states. The latter aimed to bring the armed forces of the Qajar monarchy under their own control in order to manage the situation in the country for their own benefit. The practice of using military instructors and advisers for simultaneous modernization of[46] armies of eastern countries and control over the situation in the countries and their governments was one of the means of European expansion and struggle for spheres of influence and was used in the XVIII-XX centuries quite actively. Local rulers, who either really wanted to reorganize their own armed forces to resist Europeans and have an advantage over their neighbors, or were guided by considerations of their own prestige, contributed to this. French and British instructors and advisors in the states of the Indian subcontinent before its final subjugation by Great Britain, in Iran in the first half of the 19th century, in the Ottoman Empire, German ones in the Ottoman army in the early 20th century, Russian ones in Bulgaria after the war of 1877-1878, in Korea at the end of the 19th century. - this is by no means a complete list of examples of such policies. The Qajar army at the turn of the XVIII-XIX centuries was the arena of struggle between France and England, and after the defeat of Napoleon I the place of France was taken by Russia. [47]In the late XIX - early XX centuries it was successful in this struggle: in 1879-1881 the so-called Persian Cossack Brigade (official name - His Majesty the Shah's Cossack Brigade, hereinafter - PKB) was created under the leadership of Russian officers-instructors[48] .

3. Main problems of historiography of the history of the Persian Cossack Brigade

PKB at the show and learn. In the second photo, in front on a horse V.A. Kosogovsky

After Bulgaria, Persia was the place of the most successful application of Russian military instructors in the second half of the 19th - early 20th centuries[49] . The PKB created by them existed for more than 40 years (1879 to 1920 (in 1916 it was reorganized into a division)) and, despite many problems, by the beginning of the XX century turned into a serious armed force, which eventually became the basis of the new Iranian army. In historiography the development of the Russian military-instructional mission[50] in Iran has not received comprehensive coverage. The historiographical basis for the study of the brigade's past was laid by one of its commanders, Vladimir Andreyevich Kosogovsky[51] . His "History of the PKB" is still actively, but uncritically, used by researchers of the development of the Russian military mission as almost the main source (in the broad sense of the word) for the period under consideration. Without denying the author's competence (he was in charge of the PKB for about 9 years, knew many of its commanders and officers, and was well aware of the twists and turns of its history both through oral accounts and documents of the Caucasus Military District Headquarters), it should be noted that the desire for self-glorification, obscuring some and emphasizing other moments from the history of the brigade allow us to doubt his objectivity.

Officers and "Cossacks" of the PKBU tower

PKB at the Shah's review (beginning of the XX c.)

In the future, until the beginning of the 21st century, the history of the PKB was not the object of close attention of historians. During this time, only 4 works appeared[52] , which partially or generally, but superficially considered the development of the Russian military mission.

The first of them was an extremely tendentious and devoid of historical criticism[53] work by Mikhail Pavlovich Pavlovich (Veltman), devoted primarily to the participation of the PKB in the suppression of the Persian revolution in 1908 [54] D .

The next work belonged to the British historian Firouz Kazem-zadeh[55] . It was a rather high-quality essay on the history of the PKB for that time, written on the basis of published sources. Nevertheless, the lack of archival materials (both Russian and British) makes this article valuable only from the historiographical point of view.

PKB at the review (early XX c.)

Persian "Cossacks" (early 20th century)

The other two works were written on the basis of materials from the then Soviet archives. In the first, to some extent fragmentary, work of N.R. Rikhsieva, the path of development of the Russian military mission from 1909 to 1912 was occasionally considered in a political manner. She also touched upon the events of 1893. However, N.R. Rikhsieva cited an excerpt from a document that spoke about the beginning of the crisis without any connection with the rest of the text.

Separately, it is worth noting the thesis of Nugzar Konstantinovich Ter-Oganov[56] . Considering the role of foreign military instructors in the Kajar army, he devoted a separate paragraph to the Russian military mission. He attracted new documents from the Russian State Military History Archive (hereinafter - RGVIA) (then - the Central Military History Archive of the USSR). But N.K. Ter-Oganov also followed the path suggested by V.A. Kosogovsky. In his work, he gave a sketch of the development of the PKB, starting from its scheme, without proper critical analysis.

Persian "Cossacks" in the early 20th century (the top photo shows them walking as they did in the warm season - without cherkesques).

The real boom of publications devoted to PCB began in the late 1990s[57] . Among them we should mention our works[58] , publications by N.K. Ter-Oganov and Olga

Aleksandrovna Krasnyak, as well as articles by Boris Vyacheslavovich Norik.

N.K. Ter-Oganov's work is by far the most comprehensive study on the history of the PKB. However, if the period from 1895 is studied by the author in detail, with the involvement of English Iranian sources, the time period up to 1895 is outlined schematically, without proper analysis. The author analyzed the events of May 1895 in great detail. He drew on documents unavailable to us, which established a new order of management and formation of the PKB.

O.A. Krasnyak actively used the documents of the Archive of Foreign Policy of the Russian Empire (hereinafter - AVPRI) concerning the PCRB. She reconstructed in general terms the process of the beginning of the formation of the PKB, which had been poorly studied before.

However, both authors followed the scheme proposed by V.A. Kosogovsky in the presentation of the history of the PKB of the period under consideration, so *they* reproduced all the inaccuracies and distortions of the historical material in their works.

The articles by B.V. Norik[59] stand somewhat apart. He deals with a small but important issue in the history of the PKB - the events of the first half of 1895. The researcher actively studies and pubicizes V.A. Kosogovsky's materials in the Archive of Oriental Studies of the Institute of Oriental Manuscripts of the Russian Academy of Sciences and in the Russian State Archive of Oriental Studies, in particular, his diary. Our acquaintance with the part of the "diary" kept in the RSVIA has shown that it is the diary entries that give a more objective picture of the events of 1894-1895. Using them together with other related documents of the above repositories allowed B.N. Norik to avoid being bound to the version of brigade history proposed by V.A. Kosogovsky. It remains to be hoped that this author will enrich the history of the PKB in the future with a solid monographic work devoted to the time he is studying.

Vladimir Andreyevich Kosogovsky (Kosagovsky) - Commander of the PKB 1894-1903.

Interesting publications concerning the PKB have also appeared in the West[60] . But they have a secondary character (except for the article by N.K. Ter-Oganov and U. Rabi, the main provisions of which N.K. Ter-Oganov reproduced in the book "Persian Cossack Brigade. 1879-1921"), as they are not based on historical materials in the archives of Russia and Britain, but at best on published sources. In general, the authors of these works rely on the works of each other or other scholars. Researchers either repeated the information of V.A. Kosogovsky and A.I. Domontovich, limiting themselves to general arguments for the rest, or omitted them altogether. In general, the vast majority of works are characterized by an emphasis on "popular" moments in the history of the PKB, about which there are published sources, or which were actively covered in the modern press and literature.

The exception is an extremely interesting study by Pavel Babich on V.A. Kosogovsky's views on Persia and Russia's Persian policy, based on the materials of the officer's personal fund kept in the Russian State Archive of Foreign Affairs[61] . Interestingly, the use of V.A. Kosogovsky's works allowed the author, even without a serious study of the early stage of the PKB's development, to draw some accurate conclusions regarding its place in Russian foreign policy.

PKB at the Shah's review (late 19th century)

Nevertheless, the overwhelming majority of scientific and popular scientific works, even those with a good scientific style, are characterized by many errors, inaccuracies, use of unverified information and even unconscious distortions in the presentation of the history of the PKB[62] .

First, it is the concentration of attention on "popular", "promoted" moments of the history of the PCRB, which are either covered in published sources or became the subject of political and journalistic debates. These are: the establishment of the PKB in 1878-1879 (according to the memoirs of A.I. Domontovich), the crisis of 1895 (according to the memoirs of V.A. Kosogovsky), the shooting of the Majlis and the coup of 1908. (extremely politicized in both Russian-language and English-language and Iranian historiography), and, finally, the brigade on the eve and during the First World War and its liquidation (according to published documents from the tsarist archive of the Ministry of Foreign Affairs and the memoirs of foreigners; the issue is partly politicized). A classic example is an article on the PKB in the rather authoritative Encyclopedia Iranica [63], a work on the history of the Iranian army in 1880-1917 by American historian Reza Reiss Tusi[64] and Iranian army historian Stephanie Cronin[65] .

Secondly, - the transfer of the realities of the early 20th century to the earlier history of the PKB, "tipping the present into the past"[66] , which leads to factual and theoretical errors, including in the history of the PKB.

Finally, thirdly, there is little attention to the role of personality. But, as it follows from the sources, this factor played a significant and sometimes even decisive role in the establishment and functioning of the Russian military mission in Persia. The personal opinion of the Shah (who was not known for his constancy), the position of people from his entourage, intrigues within him, the relationship of the Russian brigade commanders with Russian diplomatic representatives in Tehran and Persian dignitaries, the personal qualities of the PKB officers themselves - all these factors were, in our opinion, of primary importance in the activities of the Russian military mission.

Russian instructors and Persian officers of the PKB, 1887 (in the center - Colonel of the General Staff (hereinafter - GS) N.D. Kuzmin-Karavaev).

To exemplify these features, here are a few quotations from scientific papers with a small parsing of the errors contained in them made in footnotes.

"The Cossack brigade played an important role in the consolidation and spread of Russian influence, in Iran," noted a 1978 collective monograph. - During Nasreddin Shah's second trip to Europe in 1878, the Tsarist government managed to induce him to create a Persian Cossack brigade for the personal protection of the Shah and his family on the model of Russian Cossack regiments[67] . In 1879 the Russian government received from the Shah of Persia a firmman[68] , according to which a Persian Cossack brigade was created[69] ; officers for this brigade were sent from St. Petersburg[70] . In the same year a Russian military mission headed by Lieutenant Colonel of the General Staff A.I. Domontovich was sent to Tehran. 400 cavalrymen were allocated to create the brigade, later their number was increased. By 1880 the brigade was fully formed and consisted of two regiments. As a gift, the brigade received from the Russian government a new-style four-armed battery. The budget of the brigade was determined at 40 thousand tumans per year and was provided mainly by the revenues from the customs of Northern Iran[71] . And since all the customs of Northern Iran were actually in the hands of Russia, the salaries for officers and soldiers of the brigade were paid by the Russian government. According to the statute of the brigade it was headed by the Shah[72] , which significantly raised its prestige and put it in a privileged position in the

Iranian army[73] " .[74]

Officers of the PCB Guards Squadron

Igor Vladimirovich Bazilenko in one of his works wrote the following: "The brigade was finally formed by 1881[75] , but until the mid-1990s the Russian government paid little attention to it, recalling it only when there was a political necessity. The Persian Cossack Brigade soon became the most combat-ready part of the Iranian army, a real training school for officers, and gave Iran its first military intellectuals, including the founder of the future ruling Pahlavi dynasty (1925-1979). The brigade originally consisted of two regiments and a battery of horse artillery[76] . Officially it was called "His Majesty the Shah's Brigade". It was headed by the "head of Persian cavalry training". This position was usually occupied by a Russian colonel of the General Staff, who was appointed, with the approval of the Minister of War and the Emperor, by the military commanders of the Caucasus Military District. He was directly subordinate to the Shah and the Minister of War, but he also depended on the Russian envoy in Teheran, with whom he had to coordinate all his actions, and from whom he received constant instructions. Reports were sent to the headquarters of the Caucasus Military District. In addition to the commander, the brigade had three to five military instructors from ober-officials of the Terek and Kuban Cossack troops[77] . The instructors received salaries according to the staff from the Russian government and from the Iranian government - depending on the favor of the Shah"[78] .

Persian PKB officers (Asadollah Hosseinpour in the first photo, Reza Khan in the center background in the second photo

)

"In 1879, the main combat-ready military unit of the Persian army was the Special Cossack Brigade[79] ," wrote another contemporary Russian historian, "formed by decree of Emperor Alexander II at the request of the Shah[80] . The backbone of the brigade was made up of Russian officers[81] "[82] .

Persian officers of the 1st Cossack regiment of His Majesty the Shah. 1890 KGIAMZ

Persian officer of the PKB (early 20th c.)

The 7th volume of the Cambridge History of Iran, published in 2008, noted that "after his (Nasreddin Shah - O.G.) trip to Russia in 1878, the Shah was impressed by the Russian Cossack troops, and requested Russian officers to command and train in a new way the Persian Cossack Division[83] , which was founded in 1879. It soon became the only well-trained and reliable part of the Persian army (more than 2,000 men in the 1890s[84]), useful mainly for the defense of the Shah and his government. It was also another instrument of Russian influence in Iran" .

Mozaffar al-Din Shah and his entourage (on the right in a wide papakha - V.A. Kosogovsky; next to him - a boy in a PKB uniform) (late XIX c.)

By the lantern in a wide papakha - V.A. Kosogovsky

Ludmila Mikhailovna Kulagina gave a significant place to the essay on the PCB in her 2010 paper. It is the most adequate, compared to other "generalizations", to outline the main points of the history of the PKB. Although the essay is based on archival material, it is also not free from inaccuracies. "An important role in consolidating and spreading Russian influence in Iran was played by the Cossack Brigade," she wrote. - After the second European tour in 1878, during Nasreddin Shah's journey through the Transcaspian region[86] he was accompanied everywhere by a unit of Russian Cossacks[87] . Their horsemanship, organization, and bright uniforms made a positive impression on the Shah, and he expressed a desire to organize a cavalry unit in his army on the model of Russian Cossack regiments for personal protection.

The Cossack Brigade was organized on the basis of the Convention of 1879 between the Russian government and Nasreddin Shah. The Cossack Brigade was organized on the basis of the 1879 Convention between the Russian government and Nasreddin Shah. The purpose of the establishment of this military unit with Russian officers at its head was defined in the Convention: "The commander of the brigade should direct his strength, diligence and knowledge to the formation of a reliable and loyal military unit from the men under his command, ready to serve His Majesty the Shah at all times". In the same year Russia sent to Tehran a military mission headed by Colonel A.I. Domontovich, consisting of 3 officers and 5 outriders. To create the brigade Iran allocated 400 horsemen of irregular cavalry, later their number was increased. By 1880 the brigade was fully formed. As a gift, the brigade received from the Russian government a battery of four guns of the 1877 model. With the support of the Russian envoy I.A. Zinoviev, Domontovich organized the unit, trained it and presented it to the Shah at the end of 1879. The brigade immediately won Nasreddin's approval. In 1894, Russian officer V.A. Kosogovsky became the commander of the brigade, who did much to raise the brigade's prestige. By creating a Cossack brigade under the command of Russian officers, the Russian government primarily hoped to increase its influence on the Shah and the ruling circles of Iran and strengthen its position in the country[89] . According to its official status, the Cossack Brigade was under the jurisdiction of the Sadrazam until 1909[90] . In connection with the adoption of the constitution and the establishment of the Majlis, the convention of the brigade was confirmed by the new Iranian government with only a change in its subordination. Now the Cossack Brigade was subordinate to the Iranian Minister of War[91] . The brigade was the personal guard of the Shah and his entourage, carried out all his orders, guarded order, accompanied the Shah on trips[92] . In summer, the brigade guarded foreign missions in Shimran. The brigade's detachment from the bulk of the Iranian population made it extremely unpopular in Iran[93] . Although formally under the authority of the Iranian authorities, the Cossack Brigade was often quite independent in its activities. The Cossack Brigade was controlled by the Russian Minister of War, in wartime it was subordinated to the headquarters of the Caucasus District[94] . The brigade's activities in Iran were directly controlled by the Russian Embassy in Tehran, and the appointment of the brigade's leadership depended on it[95] . The subordination of the Cossack Brigade to the Russian authorities caused discontent of the Iranian government, which saw it primarily as a foreign military unit, imposed on Iran and unsuitable for service inside the country[96] , - maintaining order in the provinces, guarding trade routes, assisting government agencies in the collection of taxes, etc.[97] . Russian officers serving in the brigade were simultaneously on active duty in Russia, not in the reserve. In order to eliminate disagreements with the Iranian authorities, it was decided that Russian officers would serve under a contract that was concluded in Iran with all foreign instructors. When recruiting officers for the brigade, the Russian command set certain conditions[98] : experience of service in the Caucasus or Central

Asian region, minimum knowledge of Persian language, knowledge of French or other European language, familiarity with the East and Eastern customs. One of the pressing issues was the Russian lower ranks of the brigade, in particular the uriadniks. They came to Iran for an indefinite period of time[99] and were in a privileged position compared to the Iranian staff of the brigade. They took advantage of their position and sometimes abused it, which caused animosity towards them among Iranians. The rangers rarely changed, they usually came with their families and settled down for many years. They were accused of poor organization of military training of Iranians[100] ..... The Cossack Brigade did not report its financial expenditures to the Iranian government, it operated uncontrollably, which caused repeated protests from the Iranian government[101] . The brigade's reports were first submitted to the Minister of War and the General Treasury in 1913[102] , giving accounts from 1909 onwards"[103] .

PKB musicians

In the work of Gennady Vladimirovich Potapov wrote the following: "in 1879 ... on the basis of a convention between the Russian government and Nasreddin Shah, the PKB was created, which was the most capable military unit in the Iranian army. Although, according to the statute of the brigade, it was headed by the Shahanshah[104] , it was actually subordinated to the Russian Minister of War, and in wartime - to the headquarters of the Caucasus district. The brigade was commanded by a Russian officer, usually a colonel of the GSH. Senior officers were sent from St. Petersburg, and they remained on active service in Russia. The brigade consisted of two regiments, numbered about 3,500 Cossacks, 40-50 Russian officers, and more than 200 Iranian officers, half of whom were only enlisted. Iranian officers, non-commissioned officers and partly even privates of the brigade were mainly composed of relatives of the Shahanshah and sons of khans. All the armament of the brigade was supplied from Russia. The budget of the PKB amounted to about 500,000 tuman per year and was provided mainly by the revenues from the customs of Northern Iran. And since all the customs in Northern Iran were in the hands of Russia, the salaries of the personnel of the brigade were paid by the Russian government"[105] . In this message the reality of 1879-1903 corresponded only to the fact that in 1879 an agreement was concluded between the governments of Iran and Russia on the training by Russian instructors of part of the Persian cavalry; that the PKB was commanded by an officer of the General Staff; that Russian officers serving in Persia were on duty in Russia; and that the brigade consisted of 2 regiments, and the armament was supplied from the Romanov Empire. All the rest are either outright inaccuracies or facts dating back to the early 20th century.

Russian instructors and Persian officers of the PKB, from 1906 to 1909 (in the center, near the boy, is Colonel of the General Staff Vladimir Platonovich Lyakhov).

Finally, in one of the latest generalizing works on world history about the PKB wrote the following: "An important role in the consolidation and spread of Russian influence in Iran was played by the Cossack brigade. During Nasreddin Shah's second trip to Europe in 1878, the Tsarist government managed to induce the Shah to create a Persian Cossack brigade modeled on Russian Cossack regiments for the personal protection of the Shah and his family[106] . According to the statute of the brigade[107] , it was headed by the Shah[108] , which significantly raised its prestige and put it in a privileged position in the Iranian army[109] " .[110]

Russian instructors officers and ranks of the Persian Cossack E.V.S. Brigade

Early twentieth century.

In his work, the modern researcher is constantly faced with theoretical developments-"stamps" that prevent a truly objective study. These "stamps" are formed by historians and form whole generations of historians, creating trends and schools in historical science. Most often they are formed in the following way: one of the historians on a small or too extensive and poorly processed material puts forward a hypothesis that finds its supporters due to its "fashionability". The supporters advertise it, by its novelty (or "Europeanness" or "Westernness") creating conditions for attracting new researchers. However, the trouble is that these researchers, especially inexperienced young scientists, getting carried away, adjust the factual material to the hypothesis, even if it contradicts it. In relation to our topic, a good example is the theory of the so-called "military revolution". Its supporters have done much to study the military history of the world. However, the theoretical construction, created in its time on a very narrow material, still dominates them, unconsciously forcing them to adjust the conclusions of their developments to the idea of "military revolution"[111] .

In the case of the PKB, unfortunately, the stamps expressed by some historians[112] , still prevail over those who write about the brigade. As a result, during the existence of the "brigade historiography" it has accumulated many inaccuracies and even gross errors, which are replicated from researcher to researcher. Solid works devoted directly to the history of the PKB were not free from them either. Nevertheless, we are far from the idea that most historians deliberately misled and mislead their readers. Rather, the reason for many inaccuracies is the careless attitude to sources and information, as well as the inexperience of researchers.

Russian officer-in-training of the PKB

Colonel E.A. Makovkin, in 1883-1885, head of training of the Persian cavalry and commander of the 1st Cossack E.V.S. Regiment.

Photo 1910-1912.

Modernization of history, emotionalism of research, essayism, preoccupation with a particular method or methodology (especially the national approach to historiography)[113] - these are the methodological shortcomings of many modern works on history. The principle of historicism is sometimes ignored[114] . In their historical constructions it is necessary to be oriented not on the national approach to historiography, but on the scientific one[115]. In methodological terms, we are supporters of the principle "from parts to general" [116]That is, we believe that in order to create this or that concept it is necessary to first study all possible sources and details, and then go to the level of generalizations. We do not share the belief, characteristic of a significant part of historiography, that one should go from the general to the particular[117]. In such an approach, most often, speculative concepts are not proved or refuted by sources or factual material, but "transform" them to suit themselves. Classic examples are the Marxist-Leninist conception of the historical process that prevailed in the USSR, the civilization approach in its simplified form, and national (nationalist) approaches to historiography. On a personal level - historiographical concepts of two outstanding scholars - Mikhail Sergeevich Grushevsky[118] and Vasily Osipovich Klyuchevsky[119]. Both of them were engaged in the study of Russian history in the broad sense of the word, as well as the study of the history of their peoples. V.O. Kliuchevsky proceeded not from ideological constructions (although partly liberalism and Eurocentrism influenced his concept) and theoretical constructions, but from concrete-factual material and sources, on their basis moving to generalizations[120]. M.S. Grushevsky, on the other hand, was initially "blindsided" by the national idea, as a result of which he "adjusted" the factual material and information from sources to speculative, initially set conclusions, creating a historical and mythological concept of Ukraine-Rus. The concept of periodization of world history based on the history of Europe into ancient, medieval, new and modern is no less indicative. As the study of the historical process outside Europe shows, this chronology works only partially - in relation to the New (but only not from the XV century, but from the XIX century) and Modern times. The same applies to the historiographies of "nation-building" in the modern post-Soviet space. Here, the national approach and the ideological stamps associated with it make historians willingly or unwillingly adapt, "adjust" the historical material to them[121].

In the Persian Cossack E.V.S. Brigade. *From left to right:* telegraph operator, Lieutenant Blumer, Hesaul Assisr (standing), Hesaul Makovkin, Russian diplomat. The inscription on the photograph "Farewell". Tehran, 1890 KGIAMZ. The names of the officers in the order shown in the photo were established by P.N. Strelianov (Kalabukhov)

Instructor of PKB in the late XIX-early XX centuries. Afako Patsievich Fidarov

Russian instructors and Persian PKB officers in early 1921.

One cannot fully agree with Alexander Nikolaevich Bokhanov's opinion that objective historical research is impossible in principle[122] . No doubt, any research is subjective, since it is written by one or another person with his or her own perceptions and views. But the objectivity of historical research is to restore the objective historical reality, the event line at a certain period of time, indicating the reasons that caused it and formed and moved it (including the views and perceptions of the world of people involved in the events and their shaping), and, accordingly, how they influenced the course of events, based on their own perceptions. The objectivity of historical research also includes the study of the perception of contemporaries and descendants about this or that historical fact or event line, how their vision and perception of events changed, how these changes influenced the course, coverage and presentation of historical material (people's perceptions, event-causes, general historical context → historical fact (event line) θ perception and interpretation by contemporaries and descendants). Such a research implies the use of as many methods and techniques of historical and other sciences as possible, as well as the maximum number of sources and the ability to interpret them (external and internal criticism, etc.). A scientist should take into account the factor of God. Of course, the divine will can neither be interpreted nor foreseen, but it is undoubtedly present in all events of this world, and the spiritual component in all its manifestations is an important factor in the historical process. A significant indicator of the objectivity of the research is also the fact that its author does not take any of the positions of participants and interpreters of events or does not declare his methodology to be the only correct one. The scholar should also avoid, as far as possible, personal assessments[123] . Finally, he should remember that the comprehension of objective historical reality is an ongoing process. Of course, only a few historians are capable of such a study. However, this is what one should strive for.

The above remarks seem to us to be important for a possible accurate reconstruction of the history of the PKB. The history of the PKB should be studied on their basis in two directions. The first is the internal life of the brigade, the history of its development as a whole and of its individual components. This includes the so-called "microhistory" of the PKB, peculiarities of military life, etc. The second direction involves the study of the history of the PKB. The second direction involves the study of the history of the PKB, putting its internal life into the internal Persian, foreign policy and international contexts.

Conclusion

In recent decades, there have been many works devoted to Russian-Iranian relations. But they are mainly focused on the topics of relations in trade, economy, politics, culture, etc.[124] . At the same time, there are very few studies based on a comparative analysis of the two states and the world-systems they created[125] . This is especially true for Iran of the Qajar dynasty.

With these articles we tried to raise the question of the need for a deeper and more detailed comparison of Russia and Iran as two traditional states and civilizations that have responded differently to the challenges of modernization. In particular, it concerned the improvement of the armed forces. Thus, the issue of comparing the effectiveness of military instructors in Iran and military reforms in the two countries (given that in Russia they were systematically and systematically carried out since the beginning of the 18th century) requires serious study. On the example of the historiography of the PKB, we tried to point out that, despite many publications, the history of the PKB is studied superficially or fragmentarily. This remark is true for the whole topic stated in the title of our work.

References

[1] The author of this work does not claim copyright for the photos presented in the collection. All of them are freely available and taken by us from the Internet. Exceptions are a few photos provided by Pavel Nikolayevich Strelianov (Kalabukhov) or copied from his works. Some of the photos of the Persian Cossack Brigade were taken by Anton Vasilievich Sevryugin [http://aniv.ru/archive/41/antuan-sevrjugin-obraz-epohi-kadzharov-ulrike-krasberg/].

[2] Lieven D. The Russian Empire and its enemies from the XVI century to the present day. Moscow: Europe, 2007. 688 p.; Russian Empire in Comparative Perspective: Collection of articles. Moscow: Novoye Izdvo, 2004. 384 c.

By Iran we will understand the state of the late 18th - early 20th centuries. There is a more extended interpretation of Iran as the country of the Aryans, the Iranian world - "Aryanam vaija", i.e. "Aryan expanse", in the words of the Avesta, or Eranshahr, to use a later term of the Sassanid era. The eastern part of this "expanse" included almost the whole territory of present Central Asia and Afghanistan up to India. The dividing line between the east and west of the Iranian world was the desert strip of Dasht-i-Kavir and Dasht-i-Lut, stretching from the Caspian Gate near Semnan in the north to Baluchistan in the south" [Asatryan G.S.S.]. [Asatryan G.S. Ethnic Composition of Iran: From the "Aryan Space" to the Azerbaijani Myth. Yerevan: Caucasian Center of Iranian Studies. 2012. C. 13; Bartold V.V.. Historical and geographical review of Iran // Works on historical geography and history of Iran. Moscow: Oriental Literature, 2003. C. 31-228]. The name "Qajar" is associated with the dynasty of the Turkic tribe of Qajars that ruled in Iran from 1795 to 1925.

[4] Empire in our understanding is a natural stage in the development of the state, which is its highest stage. There are other concepts of this phenomenon, considering the empire simply as one of the variants of the state. In this article, an empire is a large state formation created by joining (peacefully or, more often, militarily) previously independent territories (countries and peoples) to the original core, where the central power is concentrated, and uniting them around a single political center under the aegis of a universal idea of civilizational, religious, ideological, sometimes economic nature [Theory and Methodology of Historical Science. Terminological dictionary. Edited by A.O. Chubaryan. M., 2014. C. 124-126].

[5] Grand Duke of Moscow from 1462 to 1505, sovereign of all Russia: "John, by God's grace sovereign and Grand Duke of all Russia, Vladimir, Moscow, Novgorod, Pskov, Tver, Perm, Yugra and Bulgarian and others" [Borisov N. Ivan III. M.: Molodaya Gvardiya, 2006. 691 p.; Skrynnikov R.G. Ivan III. M.: ACT, 2006. 290 c.].

[6] Both in Russia and in the lands of the Eastern Slavs that were part of the Polish-Lithuanian Commonwealth, the population called themselves Russians (Rusyns, Ruski, Ruski). Therefore, naturally in the Polish state (formally the Polish-Lithuanian Commonwealth was a multinational state, an empire-republic, but the dominant position of Poles, the Polish language and Catholicism allows us to speak of it as a Polish state in the broad sense of the word) could not call the neighboring state by its real name, as it would delegitimize the power of Poles over their Russian population. And since Western Europe got acquainted with Russia through Poland, the Latinized name "Moscovia" took root there [Karnaukhov D.V. Historical image of Moscovia in Polish chronography of the Renaissance // Bulletin of the Russian State University for the Humanities. Series "Cultural Studies. Art History. Museology". 2008. № 10. C. 101-114; Kudryavtsev O.F. Russia in the first half of the XVI century: a view from Europe. Moscow: Russian World, 1997. 408 p.; Khoroshkevich A.L. Russia and Moscovia. From the history of political and geographical terminology // Acta Baltico-slavica. 1976. VOL. X. PP. 47-57].

[7] Boev E.B. Ideology of state nationalism in Iran during the Pahlavi dynasty (1925-1979). Diss. ... Cand. hist. nauk.Nizhny Novgorod, 2017. C. 2752; Fry R. The Heritage of Iran. Moscow: Oriental

Literature, 2002. 464 c.

Lurie S.V. From ancient Rome to Russia of the XX century: continuity of the imperial tradition [Electronic resource]. Mode of access: http://ecsocman.hse.ru/data/020/073/1218/013Luoe.pdf. Partly the title of Grand Duke also can be considered as a symbol of the supreme authority as in it embodied seniority in a sort Rurikovich and, accordingly, among other Princes on Russian grounds.

[9] Surguladze V.Sh. Facets of Russian self-consciousness. Empire, National Consciousness, Messianism and Byzantism of Russia. MOSCOW: W. Baling, 2010. 480 p.; Trepavlov V.V.. The White Tsar. Image of the Monarch and the Representation of Subjection in the Peoples of Russia of the XV-XVIII Centuries. Moscow: Oriental Literature of the Russian Academy of Sciences, 2007. 255 c.

[10] If Ivan III took as a basis the Byzantine model of empire (or even wider - the Roman one, since "tsar" is a derivative of "Caesar", "Caesar", as rulers were called in the Western and Eastern Roman empires [Gorsky A.A. About the title "tsar" in medieval Russia (up to the middle of the XVI century) // Odyssey. Man in History. 1996. C. 205-211; Filiushkin A.I. Terms "tsar" and "tsardom" in Russia // Voprosy istorii. 1997. № 2. C. 144-148]), reflected also in the title "tsar", then Peter I - the Western European, also leading its tradition to ancient Rome, but a slightly different model, which was expressed in his adoption of the title "emperor".

[11] However, given the special role of "marriage diplomacy" in history, starting from *the* ancient world, such a phenomenon was the norm. It would be unusual if the dynasty was ethnically "pure". The Qajars appointed as heirs princes of the blood, i.e., those born of the ruler and a Qajar woman. But given the ethnic diversity of the harem, the relatives (even brothers, as in the case of Nasreddin Shah's sons) of the future Shah were of ethnically mixed blood. However, this was not the main thing. The main thing was to observe the principle of succession to avoid bloody struggle for power.

[12] Asatryan G.S. Ethnic Composition of Iran: From "Aryan Space" to Azerbaijani Myth. Yerevan: Caucasian Center of Iranian Studies. 2012. C. 61.

[13] A Turkic dynasty that ruled in Iran 1501-1722 and 1729-1736.

[14] In particular, it manifested itself in the borrowing of earlier terminology of the state apparatus, official language (Farsi) and culture, as well as the claim to the antiquity of the imperial power, reflected in the name of the state "Iran" and the title of the ruler "Shahanshah" ("Shahanshah-i Iran vodzhud-i ala hazrat-i aghdas-i homayun"), I.P. Petrushevsky noted that the official terminology "Iran" and "Shahanshah" did not carry any national idea, and from the time of the Sassanids in West and Central Asia with these terms was associated with the theoretical idea of "world" monarchy [Petrushevsky I.P. Sketches on the history of feudal relations in Azerbaijan and Armenia in the XVI - early XIX centuries. L.: LSU Publishing House, 1949. C. 38]. "The phenomenon of Iranian monarchical nationalism has its roots in the era of the ancient Persian empires of the Achaemenids and Sassanids," noted a contemporary historian, "when in the view of Iranians the world consisted of two parts: Iran proper and the rest (Iran va an-Iran). Inherited by the Sassanid dynasty from the Hellenized Parthian Arshakid dynasty, the institution of the Shahanshah was an expression of the absolute supremacy of the reigning house. The Safavid dynasty that came to power also began to call the rulers of Iran Shahanshahs to emphasize their greatness. In the minds of Iranians, Iran was perceived as the center of the universe. Iranian ethnocentrism has long been an integral part of the worldview of the population of this country. It is no coincidence, for example, that almost a thousand years after the collapse of the Sassanid dynasty, the capital of the Safavid Empire was put on a par with the rest of the world: Esfahan - nesf-e jahan!". [Ter-Oganov N.K. From military modernization to nationalism and nation-state in Qajar Iran // History and Historians in the Context of the Time, 2015, Vol. (14), Is. 1. P. 40]. This aspiration was also manifested in the coronation of Iranian rulers. Formally it included putting on a crown (the crown of Kiani (Keiani), named after the dynasty of the first legendary kings of Persia Keianids, the founder of which is considered to be Kei-Kobad (Kei-Kubad, Kay Kavad, Kay Kavat) [Chunakova O.M. Pahlavi dictionary of Zoroastrian terms, mythical characters and mythological symbols. M.: Oriental Literature, 2004. C. 126], which belonged to Nadir

Shah, and had four feathers on it. They symbolized the power over Iran, Afghanistan, India and Central Asia and, accordingly, the claims of the Qajar Shahs. The crown itself was also a symbol-"link" with the ancient history of Iran: thus, the antiquity and continuity of power were consolidated. Only the first monarch was an exception to the rule - he was crowned with a small diadem. The second element of the coronation was the girding with a sword consecrated on the tomb of Sheikh Sefiaddin in Ardabil. This symbolized the succession of power from the Safavids and devotion to Shiism.

[15] At least formally: it was used to man the armed forces, it was used to colonize the outskirts of the empire, it was partly used to oppose foreigners.

[16] Zhigalina O.I. Ethnosocial evolution of Iranian society. Moscow: Oriental Literature, 1996. C. 40-73.

17

However, the ethno-national picture of Iran is much more complex than it is given in the simplified version presented by us [Asatryan G.S. Ethnic Composition of Iran: From the "Aryan Space" to the Azerbaijani Myth. Yerevan: Caucasian Center of Iranian Studies. 2012. 130 p.; Zhigalina O.I. Ethnosocial evolution of Iranian society. Institute of Oriental Studies of the Russian Academy of Sciences. Moscow, Oriental Literature, 1996. 264 c.]. 18

Iran did not have serfdom in its Russian version, which was actually slavery. Personally free peasants rented land from those who owned it on behalf of the state. In Russia, such a situation developed only after the abolition of serfdom in 1861.

[19] In Iran, the predominant trend in Shi'ism is that of the Shi'ites, whose adherents are called the Shi'ites-twentieth, or Isnaasharites. They represent a moderate trend in Shi'ism, in contrast to the Ismailis. Its supporters recognize as their spiritual leaders 12 imams from the family of Ali ibn Abu Talib, a cousin and one of the closest companions of the Prophet Muhammad. They believe that the twelfth Imam disappeared at a young age in 873-874. This is the so-called "hidden Imam", whose return as the Messiah (Mahdi) is still awaited by the Shi'ite twenties. They are divided into a mainstream majority and an "Alawite" minority.

Zhigalina O.I. Ethnosocial evolution of Iranian society. Institute of Oriental Studies of the Russian Academy of Sciences. Moscow, Oriental Literature, 1996. C. 67-68. For more details on nationalisms in Russia and Iran see: Boev E.B., Voronkova G.V. National policy of the Shah government of Iran in 1925-1979 years [Electronic resource]. - Mode of access: http://scjoumal.ru/articles/issn_1997-292X_2015_12-1_05.pdf; Galkina E.S. Stanovlenie natsii i puti natsionalizm v Iran [Electronic resource]. - Mode of access: vestnik.rsu.edu.ru/pdf/7_(32).pdf; Miller A.I. Imperia Romanov i nationalizm. Essays on the Methodology of Historical Research. MOSCOW: NLO, 2006. 248 p.; Constructing Nationalism in Iran: From the Qajars to the Islamic Republic. Routledge, 2017. 300 p.

21

It is striking, for example, that its army by the last quarter of the century had many common features with the Russian army of the first half of the XVIII century and with the European armies of the early modern times. However, it had no potential for further development [Krasnyak O.A.. Formation of the Iranian regular army in 1879-1921. MOSCOW: URSS, 2007. 160 c.]. 22

Under the elite we understand representatives of the management apparatus, the ruling top. 23

This does not mean that a "monetary elite" was not formed in Iran. But its role in political processes was not significant.

Firoozeh Kashani-Sabet. Frontier Fictions: Shaping the Iranian Nation, 1804-1946.1.B.Tauns, 2000. 328 p.

[25] The Qing Empire is left out of our attention, as there were no direct contradictions between it and Turkey and Iran, and with Russia only in the northeastern part of Central Asia. We also do not take into account the European powers that tried to indirectly influence the relations in the mentioned "triangle". It was only in the 19th century that Great Britain entered this combination, after which the confrontation actually transformed into a confrontation between Great Britain and Russia.

[26] Cronin S. Importing Modernity: European Military Missions to Qajar Iran // Comparative Studies in Society and History. 2008. Vol. 50. Is. 1. P. 197-226; Roy K. Military Transition in Early Modem

Asia, 1400-1750: Cavalry, Guns, Government and Ships. Las Vegas: Published by Bloomsbury Academic, 2015. 288 p.

Regular army (in Russia in the second half of the 19th century it was also called "constant", "correct" - from Latin "regularis" "having the force of a rule", "regula" - "norm, criterion, rule"), i.e. an army organized on the basis of rules, was formed in Europe and some Asian countries at the beginning of the New Age. Its distinctive features were the presence of a clear organization; charters, on which it was based, by which it was trained and which had to be strictly observed; uniformity of armament and uniforms; the presence of a trained officer and non-commissioned officer corps; a rigid vertical command hierarchy and management; constant attendance at service and systematic training; universal (i.e. regardless of tribal, clan, feudal, etc.) principle of manning. This type of armies grew out of the regular armies of various rulers of traditional society, which were based, as a rule, on the principle of rejection of feudal-tribal manning. "Regular troops," wrote the Russian Military Encyclopedia of the 1880s, "have a correct military organization and receive thorough military training"; it also noted that these troops were on duty all year round, provided with allowances from the treasury. "At present," wrote the author of the article, Colonel of the General Staff Alexander Fedorovich Rediger, "we call regular all the permanent troops, replenished on the basis of the Statute of Conscription." [Encyclopedia of Military and Naval Sciences. St. Petersburg: Tip. V. Bezobrazov and K, 1893. T. 6. C. 286]. As a rule, regular armies were created by the central government in order to oppose feudal militias or troops of other pretenders to power, first inside the country and then outside it. The creation of regular armed forces that depended on the central government took place in New Age Persia under Abbas I. (The Iranian ruler, Shahanshah of the Safavid dynasty, who ruled from 1587-1629, carried out a series of reforms. Under his rule, the state reached its highest power. About military reforms of Abbas I and Nadir Shah Afshar (Ruler of Iran in 1736-1747) see: [Arunova M.R., Ashrafyan K.Z. The State of Nadir-Shah Afshar. Moscow: Izd-e Vostochnaya Literature, 1958. C. 129-139; Babaev K. Military reform of Shah Abbas I (1587-1629) // Bulletin of Moscow University. Series History. 1973. № 1. C. 21-30; AxworthyM. The Army of Nader Shah // Iranian Studies. 2007. Vol. 40. № 5. P. 635-646]. However, later (as a rule, after the reformer's death) the regular units slowly declined, as the next rulers did not show interest in their qualitative development (improvement of weapons, organization, etc.). Shamkhalchi, Dzhezaerchi and Tufenkji militia-musketeers, which survived until the 19th century, were a kind of "splinters" of these reforms. In the early XIX century. heir to the throne Abbas-Mirza with the help of French and then British military instructors managed to create a new regular army [Alikhanov-Avarsky M. On a visit to the Shah. Sketches of Persia. Tiflis: Tip. *Ya.I.* Liberman, 1898. C. 188, 209; Kibovsky A., Egorov V. Persian regular army of the first half of the XIX century // Tseikhgauz. 1997. № 5. C. 20-25; № 6. C. 28-31; Krugov A., Nechitailov M. Persian army in the wars with Russia. 1796-1828. Moscow: Russian Knights Foundation, 2016. 248 c.]. It consisted of infantry, artillery and cavalry. A member of the French military-instructor mission - Captain Pepin trained and armed several squadrons on the model of the French regular cavalry, which made up the Iranian regular cavalry (zam-atli or savar-nezam) [Kibovsky A., Egorov V. Persian regular army of the first half of the XIX century // Tseikhgauz. 1997. № 6. C. 28-31; Ter-Oganov N. Military and foreign policy factors in the creation of the regular army in Iran in the first half of the XIX century // Canadian-American Slavic Studies. 2012. Vol. 46. № 1. P. 1-39]. Later, through the efforts of a former French officer G. Drouville, it increased to 20 squadrons. It was organized, armed and trained according to the French model. According to the plan of G. Drouville, who was personally supported by Abbas-Mirza, each squadron in the future was to become the basis for the formation of a separate cavalry regiment. However, after the French were replaced by the British in 1809, the cavalry fell into decline. The British were not interested in its development as they feared the creation of a mobile force to attack India. The second attempt to create regular cavalry units was made during the military reforms of Mirza Taghi-khan Ferahani emir-nizam emir-e kebir, the first minister of Iran in 1848-1851. They modified the regular Persian army. But the attempt to form a regiment of regular cavalry of 750 men from the Shahseven tribe, was unsuccessful [Cronin S. Armies of Qajar Iran [Electronic resource]. -

Mode of access :
http://kavehfarrokh.com/iranica/militaria/iranian-military-history-and-armies-post-islamic-era- to-1899/professor-stephanie-cronin-armies-of-qajar-iran]. The regular cavalry units were vastly inferior to the irregulars and eventually failed to take root. As a result, by the early 1880s the Iranian regular army consisted of infantry - 76 battalions-foojas (20 in 1,000 men, 1 - 900, 53 - 800, 1 - 400, 1 - 250), the authorized strength of which amounted to 63,950 men; and artillery - 20 foojas of 250 men (10 - in Azerbaijan and 10 - in Iraq, a total of 5,600 artillerymen) [Franchini. Note on the Persian army of Major-General Franchini from September 20, 1877 // SMA. 1883. Vop. 4. C. 2, 16].

[28] Iranian ruler Shahanshah of the Safavid dynasty, who ruled from 1587-1629, carried out a series of reforms. Under his rule, the state reached its greatest power. About the military reform of Abbas I see: Babaev K. Military Reform of Shah Abbas I (1587-1629) // Bulletin of Moscow University. Series History. 1973. № 1. C. 21-29. [29] Ruler of Iran in 1736-1747. About his army see: Arunova M.R., Ashrafyan K.Z. The State of Nadir-Shah Afshar. M.: Izd-e Oriental Literature, 1958. C. 129-139; Axworth M. The Army of Nader Shah // Iranian Studies. 2007. Vol. 40. № 5. P. 635-646.

30

Ter-Oganov H. Military and foreign policy factors in the creation of a regular army in Iran in the first half of the XIX century // Canadian-American Slavic Studies. 2012. Vol. 46. № 1.
P. 1-39; Ter-Oganov H.K. Creation and development of the Iranian regular army and the activities of foreign military missions in Iran in the XIX century: Author's thesis. ... Candidate of Historical Sciences. Tbilisi, 1984. 28 p.; Krugov A., Nechitailov M. Persian Army in the wars with Russia. 1796-1828. Moscow: Russian Knights Foundation, 2016. 248 p.; Rabi U., Ter-Oganov N. The Military of Qajar Iran: The Features of an Irregular Army from the Eighteenth to the Early Twentieth Century // Iranian Studies. 2012. Vol. 45. Is. 3. P. 333-354. 31

For more details about the "military revolution" see: Military Revolution in Western Europe in the XV-XVII centuries and the development of the armed forces of the Russian state, the Polish-Lithuanian Commonwealth and the Ottoman Empire: a comparative analysis [Electronic resource]. - Mode of access: http://tochka.gerodot.ru/military; McNeil W. In Pursuit of Power Technology, Armed Force and Society in the XI-XX centuries. Moscow: ID Territory of the Future, 2008. 457 p.; Nefedov S. A. Theory of Military Revolution: Half a Century Later // Izvestia Ural Federal University. Series 2. Humanities. 2013. № 3 (117). C. 134-141; Penskoy V. The Great Firearms Revolution. Moscow: Eksmo, Yauza, 2010. 448 p.; Penskoy V.V.. Military Revolution in Europe XVI-XVII centuries and its consequences // New and Modern History. 2005. № 2. C. 194-206; Penskoy V.V.. Military Revolution of XVI-XVII centuries and its study in foreign and Russian historiography of the second half of XX - beginning of XXI centuries // Scientific Vedomosti BelGU. Ser. History. Politology. Economics. 2008. №5. Vyp. 7. C. 67-73; Tsygankov, V.V.. "Military Revolution" and the formation of modern world-economy // Bulletin of NSU. Series: Pedagogy. 2009. T. 10. Vyp. 1. C. 51-61; Parker G. The military revolution. Military innovation and the rise of the West, 1500-1800. Cambridge: Cambridge University Press, 1996. 282 p. It is interesting that in Iran until the early 20th century, despite the borrowing of military models from Europe, accompanied by attempts to establish their own training of officers, production of gunpowder, rifles, cannons, they did not lead to changes in either the economic or political structure of society.

A dynasty that ruled in Iran from 1502 to 1722.

[33] The second son of Fathali Shah (ruled 1797-1834), official heir to the throne, viceroy in Iranian Azerbaijan. He actually led foreign policy, especially against Russia, tried to reorganize the armed forces of his viceroyalty according to the European model, for which he repeatedly invited English and French instructors. He died in 1833.

[34] Shahanshah of the Qajar dynasty, ruled from 1848-1896. In writing Persian names we take as a basis: Gafurov A. Name and history: on the names of Arabs, Persians, Tajiks and Turks. Moscow: Nauka, 1987. 221 c.

[35] Igamberdiev M.A. Iran in international relations of the first third of the XIX century. Samarkand: Samarkand State University named after A. Navoi, 1961 A. Navoi, 1961. C. 30.

[36] For details see: Vasiliev L.S. History of Religions of the East. Moscow: Book House University, 1999. C. 111-184; Petrushevsky I.P. Islam in Iran in VII-XV centuries. Leningrad: Izd-vo

Leningradskogo un-ta, 1966. 400 p.; Rodionov M.A. Islam classical. St. Petersburg: Petersburg Oriental Studies, 2001. 256 c.

[37] See: Vasiliev L.S. History of Religions of the East. Moscow: Book House University, 1999. C. 160-163; Kosheva S.V. Muslim law on the nature of power. Dissertation. ... Cand. jurid. nauk. Stavropol, 2001. C. 82-107; Mehdi Sanai. Political Thought in Islamic Society // Iran: Islam and Power. M.: Kraft+, 2002. C. 6-13.

[38] Bogdanov L.F. Persia in geographical, religious, domestic, commercial and administrative respect. SPb.: Pervaya Tsentr. East, electric furnace. I. Boragansky, 1909. C. 118-119; Inayat H., Loft M. Uprising of the destitute: revolt or revolution? // Rodina. 2001. № 5. C. 136. On the relations between the clergy and the Shahs see: Sketches of the New History of Iran (XIX - beginning of XX century). Moscow: Nauka, 1978. C. 43-48.

[39] Mirza Taghi-khan Ferahani yemir-nizam yemir-e kebir (literally "one who goes ahead of the army", "great leader") was the first minister of Persia in 1848-1851, initiator of a series of reforms of a secular nature. On his reforms see: Lorentz J.H.. Iran's Great Reformer of the Nineteenth Century: An Analysis of Amir Kabir's Reforms //Iranian *Studies. 1971.* Vol. 4. Is. 2/3. P. 85-103.

[40] Kuznetsova H.A. Iran in the first half of the XIX century. M.: Nauka, 1983. C. 101.

[41] Using in this case the European terminology in parallel *with the* Iranian terminology proper, it should be noted that in essence they differed somewhat. The Europeans used their own terms for the military structures of Persia, trying to bring them closer in understanding to the European reader. Even using local names, they explained them on the basis of the European models of the time. However, the reality did not always correspond to this interpretation. Because of this, confusion arose in the writings of many military men (which later also influenced researchers who were "attached" to the terminology of the sources). Since the European armies did not have a corresponding structural unit, the name was taken by analogy. For example, tumani were called divisions or corps, fouji were called battalions or regiments, emir-penja was defined as a major-general, although it was the position of the chief of tumani (actually, corps of five types), and so on.

[42] Later, the Isfahan army was also created.

[43] Fouj in the Iranian army was a military unit, which Europeans called either a regiment or a battalion.

[44] For more details on the military reform see: Anarkulova D.M. Socio-political struggle in Iran in the middle of the XIX century. Moscow: Nauka, 1983. C. 56-57. It should be noted that despite the rather detailed analysis of military reforms, Dilshot Mirzobabaevna Anarkulova has some inaccuracies, which is caused by the mixing of pre- and post-reform categories, as well as the already mentioned adherence to the terminology of sources. For example, for some reason she calls sartip a colonel, although it was the rank of a general, and equated sarkhang to a captain, while this rank corresponded to the rank of colonel. The author divided the regiments into fouji-battalions, and those, in turn, into companies, although in reality fouji was a one-battalion regiment, which consisted of 10 companies.

[45] They had a continuation in the reforms initiated in the 1870s by the military minister Husain Khan Mushir od-Dowla (discussed below). The Shah also supported them, but it was not possible to complete the reform [Ter-Oganov N.K. Persian Cossack Brigade 1879-1921 gg. Moscow: Institute of Oriental Studies of the Russian Academy of Sciences, 2012. C. 42-46].

[46] In this case - updating according to European models (synonymous terms: Europeanization, Westernization; the latter concepts also have the meaning of socio-cultural borrowing as opposed to modernization as a technical transformation in the economic, political and social spheres). For more details on the meaning of the term "modernization" see: Gavrov S. Modernization in the Name of Empire. Sociocultural Aspects of Modernization Processes in Russia. Moscow: Unitorial Urss, 2004. 352 p.; Ermakhanova S.A. Theory of Modernization: History and Modernity // Actual Problems of Socio-Economic Development: the View of Young Scientists. Novosibirsk, 2005. Section 2. C. 233247; Ermakhanova S.A. Modernization theory: history and modernity [Electronic resource]. - Mode of access: econom.nsc.ru/ieie/SMU/conference/articles/EpMaxaHOBa.doc; Poberezhnikov I.V. Transition from traditional to industrial society: theoretical and methodological problems of modernization. M.: ROSSPEN, 2006. 240 p.; Tumanova A.S. Modernization of the Russian Empire

in the XVIII - early XX centuries: traditional and new approaches // Modernization of the State. Penza: IIC PTU, 2005. C. 19-39.

[47] Except for the official name, the terms "Cossacks", "Cossack", etc., referring to the PKB, we will take in quotation marks, because its ranks (except for Russian instructors) referred to real Cossacks only externally - by clothing and training.

[48] According to the military lexicon, the brigade is more properly called a compound rather than a unit. However, since it was a unit in relation to the rest of the Persian army, we will refer to it as both a unit and a part.

[49] Later, the experience of the PKB was used to create the Mongolian Military Instruction Mission, generally also a successful project of the Russian military. On Russian military missions abroad see: Grosul V.Ya. Russia and the formation of national regular armies of Moldavia and Wallachia // Voprosy Historii. 2001. № 5. C. 141-146; Zhalsapova J.B. Mutual relations of Russia/USSR with Mongolia/MNR in the military sphere: 1911-1939. Author's abstract of the dissertation ... Candidate of Historical Sciences. Khabarovsk, 2009. C. 16-18; Zhalsapova Zh. Activity of Russian military instructors in Mongolia (1912-1916) // Vlast. 2008. № 12. C. 120-123; Kazanova Yu.V. Russian military-instructor mission in Macedonia: formation and the beginning of work (From the history of the implementation of the Murtzsteg program) // Russian collection. M. 2009. T. 6. C. 91-111; Kim Yong-soo. Russian Military Instructors in Korea and the Korean Army // Russian Collection. Moscow: Modest Kolerov, 2006. № 2. C. 218-244; Ovsyanyi N.R. Bulgarian militia and Zemskoye voskoye voskoe. To the history of civil administration and occupation in Bulgaria in 1877-78-79. St. Petersburg: Izd. Voen.-Ist. Commission of the General Staff, 1904. 175 p.; Popov I. Russia and China: 300 years on the brink of war. Moscow: OOO Izd-vo Astrel, OOO, izd-vo ACT, ZAO NII Ermak, 2004. C. 177-194; Skvoznikov A.N. Macedonia in the late XIX - early XX century - the apple of discord in the Balkans. Samara: Samar, Humanitarian Academy, 2010. C. 85-91; Falko S.V. Military-instructor mission under the leadership of Colonel K.V. Tserpitsky to the Bukhara Emirate (1884) // Pleia. 2016. Vip. 109. C. 106-115; Khokhlov A.N. D.V. Putyata and his plan to modernize the Korean army (1896-1898) // Bulletin of the Center for Korean Language and Culture. St. Petersburg: Izd-vo S.-Peterb. un-ta, 2013. Vyp. 15. C. 172-202.

[50] In literature and sources, military missions are referred to as military missions to designate a group of military personnel sent and operating in the armies of other countries. However, strictly speaking, for the 19th century it is correct to distinguish between military and military instructional missions. The former include mainly military advisers to lead the armed forces of another power, and the latter - instructors to train the army. Nevertheless, this does not exclude the possibility that together with military advisers there may be officers and junior commanders for instruction, and the head of a military instruction mission may turn into a military advisor. On this basis, in our work we will refer to the Russian instructors mainly as they were called in the sources - military mission. Accordingly, we will write the name of a military mission with a small letter - "mission" - and that of a diplomatic mission with a capital letter ("Mission"),

[51] Kosogovsky V.A. Sketch of the development of the Persian Cossack brigade // Novy Vostok. 1923. Book 4. P. 390-402; Persia at the end of the XIX century. (Diary of Gen. Kosogovsky) // Novy Vostok. 1923. Book 3. P. 446-469.

[52] We do not consider the prefaces to the publications of documents from the history of the PKB in the 1920s that appeared in the journal "Novy Vostok", because they were extremely biased and, strictly speaking, were not studies. The preface to the diary of V.A. Kosogovsky, written by G.M. Popov, can be called partly a study. But in it the author gave only a brief analysis of V.A. Kosogovsky's personality and archival materials of his fund in the manuscript department of the Institute of Oriental Studies of the USSR Academy of Sciences [From the Tehran diary of Colonel V.A. Kosogovsky. Moscow: Izd-vostochnaya lit-ra, I960. C. 3-10].

[53] It can even be rather called publicistic and propagandistic.

[54] Here he made extensive use of materials by British professor Edward Grenville Brown, published by him in 1910. This book contained a great deal of factual material, including the history of the PKB (in particular, the text of the contract for hiring Russian instructors in 1882 was published here for

the first time). But its author, not being a professional historian (and, perhaps, acting on commission), presented this material in an extremely biased manner, without the proper analysis inherent in historical research (suffice it to say that it was he who introduced the well-known forgeries - "Lyakhov's reports", which will be discussed in the last chapter). In fact, this work was a publicistic work, created on the basis of open sources and personal observations, representing a kind of "superficial cross-section" on the history of the revolution, but not a scientific study.

[55] Kazemzadeh F. The Origin and Early Development of the Persian Cossack Brigade // The American Slavic and East European Review. 1956. Vol. 15. P. 351-364.

[56] Ter-Oganov H.K.. Creation and Development of the Iranian Regular Army and the Activity of Foreign Military Missions in Iran in the XIX century. Candidate of Historical Sciences. Tbilisi, 1984. 28 c.

[57] Ter-Oganov N.K. Persian Cossack Brigade 1879-1921 gg. Moscow: Oriental Literature, 2012. 352 p.; Tokov O.A. Anti-tobacco protests in Iran and the Persian Cossack Brigade // Innovations in Technology and Education: a collection of articles of participants of the International Scientific and Practical Conference "Innovations in Technology and Education", March 18-19, 2016. Belove: Publishing house of the branch of KuzSTU in Belove; Publishing house of St. Cyril and St. Methodius University, Veliko Tarnovo, Bulgaria, 2016. Ч. 3. C. 239-242; Tokov O.A.. Armament of the Persian Cossack Brigade // Reitar. 2017. № 4 (78). C. 180-192; 2018. № 1 (79). C. 147- 157; Tokov O.A.. Quality of training of personnel and status of the Persian Cossack Brigade in 1882-1885 // Clio. 2014. № 9. C. 95-97; Tokov O.A.. To the question of the identity of the third commander of the Persian Cossack Brigade // BICHHK Lugans'kyi naschonal'nogo ushversitutu 1mesh Taras Shevchenko. 2013. № 1 (260). Ch. 2. P. 83-92; Tokov O.A.. Crisis in the Persian Cossack Brigade. 1889-1895 // Clio. 2008. № 2. C. 91-98; Tokov O. Unknown episode from the history of the "Eastern Question": the Russian military mission of 1877 to Persia // Izvestiya na institut za historicheskogo nasledeniya. Collection in honor of the pref, Dr. Stefan Doinov. Sofia: Akademichno izdatelstvo Prof. Marin Drinov 2014. T. 31. C. 115-134; Tokov O.A.. Persian Cossack Brigade in 1882-1885 // Vostok. 2014. № 4. C. 48-60; Tokov O.A.. Persian Cossack Brigade in the memoirs of A.M. Alikhanov-Avarsky // Innovations in Technology and Education: a collection of articles of participants of the VII International Scientific and Practical Conference "Innovations in Technology and Education", March 28-29, 2014. Branch of KuzSTU in Belove. Belove: Publishing House of KuzSTU Branch in Belove, Russia; Publishing House of St. Cyril and St. Methodius University, Veliko Tarnovo, Bulgaria, 2014. Ч. 4. C. 93-96; Gekov O.A.. Persian Cossack Brigade in 1878-1895: Sketches of History in the Context of the Foreign Policy of the Russian Empire concerning Iran (according to Russian sources). Saarbrücken: LAP Lambert Academic Publishing, 2017. 689 p.; Gekov O.A.. Reasons for the creation of the Persian Cossack Brigade in historiography and sources // Innovations in technology and education. Proceedings of the V International Scientific Conference: Collection of articles: In 4 parts. Belove: Publishing house of the branch of KuzSTU in Belove, 2012. Ч.
3. C. 12-15; Gekov O.A.. Russian military mission to Iran during the Russian-Turkish war of 1877-1878 // Clio. 2014. № 2. C. 90-96; Gekov O.A.. Russian officers and the Persian Cossack Brigade (1877-1894) // Canadian American Slavic Studies. 2003. Vol. 37. № 4. P. 395-414; Gekov O.A.. Russian military instructor mission in Persia under the leadership of Colonel of the General Staff N.Y. Shneur // Russian Sbornik. M., 2017. T. 21. C. 154-208; Gekov O.A.. Creation and initial stage of existence of the Persian Cossack Brigade (1879-1882). Saarbrucken: LAP Lambert Academic Publishing, 2014. 128 p.; Krasnyak O.A.. Russian military mission in Iran (1879-1917) as an instrument of Russia's foreign policy influence [Electronic resource]. Mode of access: http://www.hist.msu.ru/Science/Conf/01_2007/Krasniak.pdf; Krasnyak O.A.. Formation of the Iranian regular army in 1879-1921. M., 2007. 160 p.; Ter-Oganov N.K. Persian Cossack Brigade 1879-1921 gg. Moscow: Oriental Literature, 2012. 352 p.; Ter-Oganov N.K. Persian Cossack Brigade: the period of transformation (1894-1903) // Vostok. 2010. № 3. C. 69-79.

[58] For reasons of scientific ethics, we will not analyze our own publications, leaving this task for future researchers. We will only note that they are unequal. In our early studies, we also relied mainly on the model of the historical development of the PKB proposed by V.A. Kosogovsky and were not

critical enough of the reports of sources and literature. In recent works (also due to the emergence of new sources), we have substantially corrected our view of the history of the PKB up to the beginning of the 20th century, resulting in a series of articles and 2 monographs.

[59] Norik B.V. First steps of V.A. Kosagovsky as commander of the Persian Cossack Brigade (based on the materials of the "Diary" for 1895) // Iran-name. 2013. № 3. C. 169-177; Norik B.V. Report of Colonel V.A. Kosagovsky on the situation in the Persian Cossack Brigade. 1895 // Eastern Archive. 2018. №1.C. 20-32.

[60] Cronin S. Deserters, Converts, Cossacks and Revolutionaries: Russians in Iranian Military Service 1800-1920 // Iranian-Russian Encounters: Empires and Revolutions since 1800. Abingdon, UK and New York: Routledge, 2012. P. 143-187; Cronin S. Importing Modernity: European Military Missions to Qajar Iran // Comparative Studies in Society and History. 2008. Vol. 50. Is. 1. P. 197-226; Rabi U., Ter-Oganov N. The Russian Military Mission and the Birth of the Persian Cossack Brigade: 1879-1894 // Iranian Studies. 2009. Vol. 42. № 3. P. 445-463д

[61] Babich P. A Russian officer in Persian Cossack Brigade: Vladimir Andreevich Kosagovskii. Budapest: CEU, 2014. 84 p.

[62] This is a characteristic feature of the historiography of the entire history of the PKB. For example, let us refer only to a small episode with biographical data of the "Iranian" period of the life of one of the brigade commanders of the First World War of 1914-1918. - Colonel GS George Iosifovich Klerzhe, dismantled by A.L. Posadskov [Posadskov A.L. Liberal Colonel from Oswedverkh: labyrinths of fate G.I. Klerzhe - officer, journalist and memoirist // Klerzhe G.I. Revolution and Civil War: personal memoirs. Novosibirsk: GPNTB SB RAS, 2012. C. 10-26]. In our study, we will not consider a block of compilation, journalistic and frankly propagandistic articles that talk about the PKB. They are based on published memoirs and scientific publications and do not represent scientific value. However, it should be noted that, for example, in the Internet space, they are the ones that shape the average person's perception of the PKB. Therefore, it should be noted that the shortcomings mentioned for the works we analyze here appear in a hypertrophied form. However, since we will deal with the shortcomings of scientific works in our study, we will refrain from a separate characterization of errors and distortions made in this block of literature.

[63] Atkin M. Cossack Brigade // Encyclopedia Iranica. Vol. VI. Fasc. 3. P. 329-333 [Electronic resource]. - Access mode: http://www.iranicaonline.org/articles/cossack- brigade.

[64] Reza Ra'iss Tousi. The Persian Army, 1880-1907 // Middle Eastern Studies. 1988. Vol. 24. Is. 2. P. 219-226.

[65] Cronin S. The Army and Creation of the Pahlavi State in Iran, 1921-1926.1.B.Tauris, 1997. P. 54-107. However, the chapter on PKB covers the period from 1906 to 1921, but contains a small introduction. All the above-mentioned components are present here, with the caveat that the research focus is on the first quarter of the 20th century.

[66] In this context, we would also like to note that many historians write from today, already knowing how certain events developed. But at the same time they forget that at this or that moment in history, the way this or that process would go was not known, and there could be different variants of the course of events.

[67] Not for the Shah's personal protection - that function was performed by a detachment from the Qajar tribe.

[68] It was not the Persian government that received the firman (Shah's decree), as the firman was related to the internal affairs of the Qajar monarchy. Besides, it was not a firman, but a contract for hiring Russian instructors, which was supplemented by the Russian-Persian convention with a convention on the creation of the first cavalry unit.

[69] It was not a brigade that was created. According to the contract, the instructors were to train a part of the Persian cavalry. As a result, they initially received only a regiment (fouj) for training, and not a full regiment by Iranian standards.

[70] Officers, with few exceptions, were sent from the Caucasus Military District.

[71] Customs revenues began to be provided from the beginning of the 20th century. Initially, it was

based on muhajirs' wages (see Chapter 2 for details).

72 There was no statute of the PKB until the beginning of the 20th century. The head of the PKB was the Head of the Persian Cavalry Training Department, who was subordinate not to the Shah, but to the Iranian Minister of War.

73 The privilege did not lie in this, but in the fact that the PKB enjoyed the patronage of the Russian Diplomatic Mission and was paid a regular salary compared to the rest of the Iranian army.

74 Sketches of the New History of Iran (XIX - early XX c.). M.: Izd-vostochnaya lit-ra, 1978. C. 138.

[75] In 1880.

[76] As well as a military band and a Guards half squadron, re-formed into a squadron.

[77] The staff officers were 3 and the oberofficials were 5.

78 Bazilenko I.V. Orthodox Russia and Shiite Iran: On the pages of the history of relations (XVI - early XX cc.). C. 175-176 [Electronic resource]. - Access mode: christian-reading.info/data/2011/02/2011-02-05.pdf. This information is taken from our articles without reference to them [See, for example, Gokov O.A. Historiography of the history of the Persian Cossack Brigade // Russian History. 2006. Vol. 33. № 1. P. 63]. In the memoirs of A.I. Domontovich, to which the scientist referred, the information given by him is absent. And they received a salary from the Shah according to the contract.

The brigade was not formed until 1880, and was called His Majesty the Shah's Persian Cossack Brigade. 80

There was and could not have been any decree of the Russian Emperor on the formation of a Persian military unit in Iran. 81

The backbone of the PKB were the Muhajirs, a group of Turkic-speaking tribes that left the South Caucasus after the Russian conquest in 1829.

82 A JATT TI TI TTTTT/1/E/4L1/41 *1-1* 4 A *JAIR*\

Multatuli P.V. Foreign Policy of Emperor Nicholas II (1894-1917). MOSCOW: FIV, 2013. C. 377. 83

The division was not created until the outbreak of World War I.

84 Until the beginning of the 20th century. The PKB never exceeded 1,500 people, and even to this figure was brought only in 1899.

The Cambridge History of Iran. From Nadir shah to the Islamic republic. Cambridge University Press, 1991. Vol. 7. P. 191-192.

[86] Transcaucasian region.

[87] The researcher actually reproduced the memoirs of the first head of the Russian military mission in Tehran, A.I. Domontovich.

In 1879 a contract was signed February 7 and a convention July I to establish the first cavalry unit. It is the convention in question here. 89

The idea of inviting Russian military instructors belonged to the envoy in Tehran I.A. Zinoviev, who sought to paralyze the British influence at the Shah's court in the conditions of the struggle for the Turkmen lands. There were no far-reaching plans for the mission, but it is obvious from its history that once they had "secured" a place, they were not going to give it up.

[90] Until 1895 it was under the authority of the Minister of War, and *from* 1895. - the First Minister.

[91] In essence, it was a return to the old chain of command. Both in the case of 1895 and in this case, the decisions to re-subordinate were political in nature.

92 It acquires all these functions only at the beginning of the 20th century.

[93] Here the author follows the Iranian constitutionalists of the period of the Iranian Revolution of 1905-1911. In fact, the authority of the PKB among the ordinary population was very high: in addition to the impressive appearance of the "Cossacks," the brigade offered protection against any arbitrary rule and a stable salary. It was unpopular among those who sought to seize power in the country, socialists and nationalists.

[94] These subordination and control were only introduced during World War I.

[95] The Mission directed the activities of the Russian instructors because they were formally Russian mercenaries in the Iranian service. The role in appointing PKB commanders, however, was not comprehensive. The selection was the responsibility of the Caucasian commanders, followed by coordination with the Ministry of War and the Ministry of Foreign Affairs. The latter, at the same time, sought the opinion of the envoy in Tehran (coordination with the envoy could also begin at the level of the leadership of the Caucasus Military District).
[96] Regarding the protection of domestic order, the PKB was the only military unit that was a pillar of domestic order until 1911, when a gendarmerie under Swedish officers was established. Here again, the author repeats the accusations of the Iranian constitutionalists, which had been made against the PKB and its commander especially since 1909, and which were tacitly supported by the Anglo-American Mission. Among the Persian government circles of the last quarter of the 19th century, the attitude towards the PKB was far from unequivocal. It hindered, first of all, those who sought to overthrow the existing government.
The PKB did not acquire all these functions until the second half of the 1890s.
[98] Until the end of the century, there were no clear-cut conditions regarding candidates for instructor positions. It was emphasized only that officers should be cavalrymen or horse artillerymen, and all instructors had to wear a Cossack uniform in Iran, even if they had not served in Russia in the Cossack forces.
[99] Up to the end of the 19th century, Uryadniks came to Iran under a 3-year contract.
[100] Everything about the rangers is mainly characteristic of the late 19th and early 20th centuries, when in 1895 the restrictions on the term of Russian instructors' tenure in their posts were lifted. As for the accusations, this is again following largely emotional and unfounded accusations by Iranian constitutionalists of the period of the Iranian Revolution.
[101] Here the author also cites the accusations of the constitutionalists, which practically did not correspond to the reality of the last quarter of the 19th century. Financially, the PKB was completely dependent on the Persian Minister of War until the end of the century.
[102] For the first time in the 20th century. In the period under review, at the end of the contract, each PKB commander reported his expenses to the Iranian Minister of War and, in part, to the Russian Mission.
[103] Kulagina L.M. Russia and Iran (XIX - early XX century). Moscow: ID Klyuch S, 2010. C. 136-140.
[104] Shahanshah - "king of kings"; a title of Persian monarchs, tracing its origin to the Achaemenid dynasty (558-330 BC), whose rulers first began to call themselves by this name. It was used intermittently by various dynasties on the Iranian throne for about 2,500 years.
[105] Potapov G.V. Persian Empire. Iran *from the* most ancient times to the present day. Moscow: Algorithm, 2013. C. 262.
[106] The Shah was induced, not by the government, but by the envoy in Teheran; not to create a brigade, but to accept Russian instructors to train a part of the Persian cavalry; not to guard the Shah and his family, but to reform a part of the Iranian cavalry, or rather to shield the Iranian army from the penetration of British military instructors.
[107] There was no charter for the PCB.
[108] The PKB was headed by the Head of Persian Cavalry Training, a Russian colonel of the General Staff, subordinate to the Iranian Minister of War. Given the all-encompassing power of the Shah, we can certainly say that the PKB was subordinate to the Shah.
[109] The prestige of the PKB was raised by the patronage of the Russian Mission and the regular payment of salaries.
[110] World History: In 6 vol. Moscow: Nauka, 2014. T. 5: The World in the XIX century: on the way to industrial civilization. C. 571.
[111] The best proof of this is the uncertainty in the dating of the "military revolution", which is arbitrarily expanded and narrowed in the chronological framework, because the real material contradicts the prevailing concept, but historians cannot abandon it.

[112] Especially in a "national", pro-Iranian or anti-colonial way.

[113] An example of such fascination with the methodology of Orientalism is the interesting work of Vladimir Olegovich Bobrovnikov, devoted to a comparative analysis of the situation of Algeria and the Russian Caucasus [Bobrovnikov V. Russian Caucasus and French Algeria: accidental similarity or exchange of experience in colonial construction? // Imperium inter pares: The role of transfers in the history of the Russian Empire (1700-1917): Sb.st. Moscow: New Literary Review, 2010. C. 182-209]. Here the author, talking a lot about the imaginary, forgets that Algeria was by the beginning of the XIX century the pirate capital of the Mediterranean, and the mountaineers of the Caucasus were famous first of all for robbery raids, including for stealing people into slavery (by the way, a similar situation was in the XIX century with the Turkmen). And these were not imagination games of Russian or French authors. The images of highlanders (and Turkmens, which will be discussed separately) were formed under the influence of oriental stereotypes only partially. First of all, the forming factor was the real interaction of peoples, and the first contacts were of great importance, which often influence the formation of the image of the "other". And these contacts, as well as subsequent ones, were negative for Russians and were connected with robbery and armed raids on Russian territories. Discussing a lot about the reasons for the penetration of the Russians into the Caucasus and the French into Algeria, V.O. Bobrovnikov for some reason overlooks economic motives, but in the French case they played an important role, while in the Russian case they played a secondary one. Speaking about colonial relations, colonial character, colonization and leading readers to the idea of similarity of the two colonial empires, the researcher does not explain what he means by these terms. Pointing out that "the main feature of the colony in both cases was the native status of the population .... autonomous, disadvantaged in rights in comparison with the citizens of the metropolis or Central Russia" [Ibid. P. 198]. [Ibid. P. 198], seems extremely insufficient, since the status of the population is not the main feature of the colony, but only a secondary one. In this article we see a classic example of when a researcher in search of the imaginary uses his imagination based on an absolutized methodology, perhaps without wishing to do so himself, instead of both the researched and the real facts. When the search for the imaginary captures the researcher's imagination, and he himself begins to think for the object of study, sometimes what in fact he could not imagine. In this way, the imagination of the researcher is substituted for the imagination of the researched, which the latter passes off as the former. Another example of fascination with methodology is imperiology. In Russia and Ukraine it is vividly represented on the pages of an interesting journal "Ab imperio". But, unfortunately, in addition to the excessive fascination of many authors with "imperial motives", they suffer from another significant shortcoming - poor Russian language. Many of its articles written in Russian cannot be read without an interpreter, as they are full of largely unjustified foreign-language borrowings. Besides, literature in Russian and Cyrillic languages in general, for some reason, is transliterated rather than written in the original language. Here we have a classic example of "child" or "slave" psychology: children and slaves always want to resemble their elders/masters, so they often copy them. This would look quite funny if it were not so dangerous for the development of science. Many authors of essays on imperial themes are so caught up in the novelty or fashion of the approach that they see imperial motifs in any event or phenomenon, and use the terms "empire," "imperial," "imperialism," etc. both for business and pleasure [e.g., Martin W. Barymta: Custom in the eyes of nomads, crime in the eyes of the empire // Russian Empire in foreign historiography. Works of recent years: Anthology. Moscow: New Publishing House, 2005. C. 360-391].

[114] The principle of considering the world, natural and socio-cultural phenomena in the dynamics of their change, formation in time, in a regular historical development, assuming the analysis of research objects in connection with the specific historical conditions of their existence. There are other close definitions: 1) one of the principles of historical cognition, requiring any historical event to study in development and taking into account the specific situation; 2) the basis of historical consciousness, assuming the distinction between the past and the present, compliance with the historical context and perception of history as a process, indicating specific ways to extract useful knowledge in the course of scientific historical research [Theory and Methodology of Historical Science. Terminological

dictionary. M.Aquilon, 2014. C. 149- 151; Bargh M. Epochs and Ideas. Formation of historicism. Moscow: Mysl, 1987. 354 p.; Goryunkov S.V. Historism: the crisis of the concept and ways to overcome it // Electronic Journal "Knowledge. Understanding. Mindfulness". 2010. No. 4 [Electronic resource]. - Access mode: http://www.zpu-joumal.ru/e-zpu/2010/4/Goriunkov/; Kuznetsova T.F. Historism and thesaurus analysis of culture // Electronic journal "Znanie. Understanding. Mindfulness". 2008. № 9. [Electronic resource]. - Access mode: http://www.zpu-joumal.ru/e-zpu/2008/9/Kuznetsova].

[115] In terms of national history, for example, the Russo-Japanese War of 1904-1905. - is a tragic failure of Russia. From the point of view of scientific history, it is an episode of struggle of the major powers of the world for its redistribution, which ended in success for one and failure for the other. Similarly, from the scientific point of view, the name "Azerbaijani state of Safavids" is meaningless. [Jafarli N. Azerbaijan Safavid State. Izd-v. R. Aslanov "Legal Center Press", 2009. 254 p.; Efendiyev O. Azerbaijan Safavid State in XVI century. Baku: Elm, 1981. 335 p.], as at that time there were no Azerbaijanis as a nation; moreover, the association was not on ethnic but on religious level. Besides, the central idea of the Eranshahr state was the idea of "Iran-empire" and "Iranians" as inhabitants of this empire and Shiites. We will try, adhering to the scientific approach, to consider the history of PKB through the prism of Russian interests. We deliberately do not use the term "national interests" as it has a propagandistic rather than scientific character. We are also against the personalization of states. History was made not by abstract soulless constructions like "government", "Russia", "Iran", etc., but by living people with their characters, beliefs, personal initiative, advantages and disadvantages. A state is, first of all, a group of people who are in power by virtue of the principles of force or tradition and who dictate their will, their vision of society's development to the rest of its part or construct them in the heads of the subordinates. Therefore, it is more correct to speak not about national interests or interests of Russia, but about the interests of its ruling elite, certain individuals or strata of the population. If somewhere in the text we will use personified notions like "Russia decided", "England thought", etc., we will imply exactly the above interpretation.

[116] In our opinion, any historiographic and source methodology carries a certain cognitive charge. But it should not be absolutized, otherwise its value is sharply reduced. The best example of this is the nationalist/nationalist approach to historiography, in which myths sometimes substitute reality and force historians to fit sources to an imaginary "calque".

[117] In modern historiography, due to the dominance of this principle, studies based not on sources but on the beliefs of the authors dominate.

[118] Grushevsky M. 1storlya Ukrausha-Pyci. Kπϊβ: Naukova Dumka, 1991. T. 1. 736 c; 1992. T. 2. 640 c; 1993. T. 3. 592 p.; Vol. 4. 544 c; 1994. T. 5. 704 c; 1995. T. 6. 680 p.; Vol. 7. 628 s; Th. 8. 856 c.; 1996. T. 9. Book 1. 880 c.; 1997. T. 9. Book. 2. 776 p.; 1998. T. 10. 408 c; 2000. T. 11: Pokazhchik 1men. 520 c.

[119] Klyuchevsky V.O. Course of Russian History // Works in 9 vol. Moscow: Mysl, 1987. T. 1. 430 p.; Vol. 2. 447 c.; 1988. T. 3. 414 c.; 1989. T. 4. 398 p.; Vol. 5. 476 c.

120

However, at the same time, his reasoning retained a large share of Eurocentrism: he analyzed most of the processes of Russian history through the prism of Western European ideas and institutions contemporary to him. He paid little attention to the religious background of the events of Russian history.

Bordyugov G.A., Bukharaev V.M. Yesterday's Tomorrow: How "national histories" were written in the USSR and how they are written now. M.: АПРО-XXI, 2011. 248 p.; World War II and the Great Patriotic War in the history textbooks of the CIS and EU countries: problems, approaches, interpretations // Problems of National Strategy. 2010. № 3 (4). C. 162-185; The Baltic States and Central Asia within the Russian Empire and the USSR: myths of modern textbooks of post-Soviet countries and the reality of socio-economic calculations. Moscow: Center for Public Technologies, 2009. 199 p.; Ferro M. How History is Told to Children in Different Countries of the World. M.: Vysshaya shkola, 1992. 351 c. 122 TI ATTTCH'-' U' AX>"<T;Г-ГI/■Λ/ 'X-IΛ I-Λ T"u

Bokhanov A.H. Russian Empire image and meaning. MOSCOW: FIV, 2012. C. 13. Works such as his are based mainly on philosophical speculations of various thinkers such as N.A. Berdyaev, V.S. Solovyov, K.N. Leontiev, etc., which reflected not the realities of life, but their own ideas about these realities. These ideas were based, most often, not on personal knowledge and experience, on scientific research, but on their own speculative constructions. Therefore, the use of the works of such thinkers as a characterization of the Russian mentality, the "Russian world", the peculiarities of the Russian people, etc. from a scientific point of view should not be comprehensive (as in the case of authors like A.N. Bokhanov), but of a point character. The works of philosophers reflect mainly the worldview of themselves, a small part of the people - intellectuals, who transfer their own fantasies without supporting them with proper research material to the entire Russian people and speak on its behalf. It is characteristic that in imperial Russia there were at least two cultures - the upper and the lower - which differed from each other to such an extent that their representatives did not understand each other. The best proof of this is the revolution and civil war in Russia at the beginning of the 20th century, when some intellectuals, such as I.A. Bunin, were filled with anger towards the common people, and some were mired in abstract speculative reasoning. At the same time, the Bolsheviks understood the people's needs better than anyone else and used this understanding for their own purposes).

[123] As an example of two approaches - subjective and close to objective - we can cite 2 works on the history of Russian foreign policy under Emperor Nicholas II [Multatuli P.V. Foreign Policy of Emperor Nicholas II (1894-1917). MOSCOW: FIV, 2013. 840 c. and Rybacheonok I.S. Zakat great power. Foreign policy of Russia at the turn of XIX-XX centuries: goals, tasks, methods. M.: ROSSPEN, 2012. 582 c. respectively].

[124] Among the latter it should be noted: Bazilenko I.V. Ocherki istorii istorii russko-iranskikh otnosheniya russko-iranskikh otnosheniya (late XVI - early XX c.). SPb.: Argus, 2017. 432 p.; Kulagina L.M. Russia and Iran (XIX - early XX century). Moscow: ID Klyuch S, 2010. 271 p.; Atkin M. Russia and Iran, 1780- 1828. Minneapolis: Minnesota Archive Editions, 1980. 232 p.; Iranian-Russian Encounters: Empires and Revolutions Since 1800. UK and New York: Routledge, 2012. 411 p.; Russians in Iran: diplomacy and power in the Qajar era and beyond. I.B.Tauris & Co. Ltd. 288 p.

[125] Bazilenko I.V. Russia - Iran: History of Relations and Evolution of Religious Ideas (late XVI century - early XX century). Saarbrucken, 2012. 308 c.

Printed by Books on Demand GmbH, Norderstedt / Germany